LOSING HIM GAINING YOU

DIVORCE AS OPPORTUNITY

CORBIN LEWARS

Booktrope Editions
Seattle WA 2014

Cover Design by Loretta Matson

Edited by Joanna Dyer
& Christine Johnson-Duell

Previously Published as *Divorce as Opportunity*, 2013

PRINT ISBN 978-1-62015-344-4

EPUB ISBN 978-1-62015-369-7

For further information regarding permissions, please contact info@booktrope.com.

Library of Congress Control Number: 2014903269

*This book is dedicated with love and gratitude
to all of my present and future divorce buddies.*

CONTENTS

INTRODUCTION

WHEN I WAS IN FIFTH GRADE, my classmates concocted a game called "wedding." A girl picked a bouquet of clovers and stood with a boy in front of a fifth-grade minister. "Love and obey" and other such terms were pronounced by said minister, and then the boy and girl chastely kissed. Or giggled. Or ran.

When it was my turn to play wedding, I ran. Not at the kissing part, but before the game even began. I viewed the game as a recess disruption—an icky one at that. I merely wanted to play kickball. I spent every recess for an entire week running from a dozen fifth graders who wanted me to hold the bouquet. They eventually gave up on me, and I was able to resume my own games in peace.

I entered my teen years and twenties with similar nonchalance about weddings, but by then I liked boys. I was constantly in love and in a relationship, but I never fantasized about what kind of wedding dress I would wear or what the ceremony would look like. To this day, I've never seen the inside of a *Bride* magazine or a bridal shop.

By the time I was twenty-three, I had lived with several of my boyfriends. Cohabitating was more a pragmatic gesture than a statement of proposed longevity, and most of these relationships ended within months. I assumed the same things would happen when I dated—and then promptly moved in with—my boyfriend Jeremy. After seven years of living together, our family and friends all wondered why we hadn't gotten married. I believe my response was, "Why would we do that?" It wasn't that I was afraid of commitment—we already owned a home together and I wanted to have children with him—I just didn't see the need for a wedding to validate that commitment. We discussed it for months, warmed to the idea of a "big party," and eventually I bought a $40 dress and we were married in our backyard.

Although I was not someone who cried during romantic movies or weddings, I did believe in love. Love was my religion. I believed love above all else was what was important. And as long as I had love, I deemed my relationship to be in good standing.

I also believed in family. I embraced the value of *chosen* family and didn't believe a marriage or even ties of blood were necessary to create a family. My closest friend of twenty years was a single mom who put herself through college and graduate school while also raising her son. I idolized her and always viewed her and her son as a family. Yet when my marriage started to falter, I never thought my kids and I could be a similar family on our own. Instead I fixated on the "broken" part of "broken family." A deeper belief guided me: *You don't break up a family.* And my family included my husband.

I can't blame a devout religious upbringing or even anti-divorce parents or relatives for these ingrained beliefs. I came up with them all on my own, and I had no idea I even had them. The ideals that I spoke of and recommended for other women were not those I followed myself. Somewhere along the way, I renounced choice and options for myself. Even worse, I negated my true feelings. I had a kind husband, two healthy and smart children, and a beautiful home, so I must be happy, right? This was what I wanted, so I would make it work.

For years, the Beatles song "All You Need Is Love" played incessantly in my head. It assuaged my concern and displeasure with my marriage. "We never spend time together," I worried, but John Lennon's voice soothed that troubling thought. I was incredibly lonely, but I negated that feeling by telling myself that loneliness was impossible. "You have a family, how can you be lonely?" But Jeremy and I were often depressed, we ignored one another, and the resentments built, though I didn't want to see it. And even when I was finally willing to admit my marriage was in trouble, I told myself the only solution was to fix it. The idea of divorce didn't enter my mind; the "families are forever" belief was too strong a force.

Love and hope, mixed with denial, kept me in my marriage for years. We tried counseling, which worked for a while but eventually revealed that my marriage had even more problems than I'd thought. Our relationship had been based around ease and autonomy. This worked well when we were twenty-four and our biggest concern was which band to hear that evening, but it didn't provide the foundation needed for an adult relationship. We didn't come together to make decisions and plan for our future; we worked separately. We had different approaches to problem solving and different goals and outlooks. We even had separate friends. Our younger selves still liked and even loved one another, but our thirty-eight-year-old selves didn't *know* one another. And when we tried to get to know each other, we realized we were no longer compatible.

But I still didn't think about getting divorced. Instead, I relied on friends to fill the emotional needs that weren't met in my marriage. Eventually, that wasn't enough. One rainy day I showed up on my friend Erika's doorstep and announced, "I can't do this anymore." I had no idea what "not doing this" looked like, but I knew "this" wasn't possible anymore. Although I felt devastated, exhausted, and scared, a tiny crevice opened up in my brain that day.

Being attached to "families are forever" had left me feeling trapped and powerless. I'd felt I didn't have an option except to try to improve my marriage. But when I left Erika's house, the powerless feeling switched to a sense of possibility: "Maybe I don't have to try anymore. Maybe I have other options. And maybe, just maybe, they will be better than this."

Jeremy and I separated, and hope started to replace denial. This time my hope wasn't that my marriage would improve or Jeremy would change; it was hope that I would be all right—no matter what. I realized by placing all of my hope and focus on Jeremy, I had been negating myself and my children, so I redirected the focus to myself. Hope turned to faith, and with that, I asked for a divorce.

Yes, I was devastated to break up my children's nuclear family, heartbroken to lose Jeremy, and terrified about how I would financially and emotionally survive. But amongst all of the sadness and turmoil was a new sense of opportunity. For nearly six years, I had tried the same tactics, expecting different results. According to Einstein, this is the definition of insanity. Now I was trying something new, and that was a huge relief. I wrote the word "Opportunity" in bright colors and placed the card in my bathroom mirror. Whenever fear threatened to immobilize me, I looked at that card and remembered I had options.

While struggling with my marriage, I had shared my deepest feelings only with a couple of friends. Once I separated, I wanted to talk to everyone about my upcoming divorce. People's first response was almost always, "I'm sorry about your failed marriage." I'd reply, "Don't be. It was a success for most of the fourteen years. And I view it as an even better success that we knew how to end it before it became damaging."

I started seeking out other divorced women to talk to about my divorce, and they rarely said, "I'm sorry." Instead, they nodded. They understood that a divorce isn't really about a failed marriage; it's about a need for change. These women provided emotional and physical support, friendship, love, a renewed sense of family, and proof that my kids and I would be all right. "You'll be better than all right," one of them said. "You'll be fabulous."

I subsequently learned from a study conducted in 2000 that women are the majority of initiators and filers for divorce—up to 80% in some states and Canada. Furthermore, the number one reason women gave for wanting a divorce was the husband's inability or lack of desire to grow and change. The majority of the women revealed that they are happier divorced than they were while married, and that they were certain that leaving their marriages was the right thing.[1]

Yes, divorce is hard—but we all know that. What we don't necessarily know is that divorce can bring amazing opportunities, change, and growth. As Jessica Bram, the author of *Happily Ever Divorce,* says, "But here's a radical thought—what if someone had told me I might not end up poor after my divorce, that my sons would thrive, and my life would become a thousandfold better than it had ever been before? That I would grow in ways I could never imagine?"

I wrote this book with the hope that I could help ease the decision for other women by sharing my experience as well as the experiences of others. I talked to numerous women, and some men, all of who were in the midst of divorce or recently divorced. With time, almost all of the people I talked to were able to make positive changes in their life. Many of them excelled in their careers, gained confidence in themselves and their abilities, and raised kids who have thrived in two homes. Substantial research has shown that the key to children's psychological well-being is the level of conflict between the parents, not whether the parents remain married.2 Divorce itself doesn't harm children— angry, resentful, unhappy parents harm children. And feeling trapped harms everyone. I hope these stories will allow you to believe you have options and hope as well.

Divorce is not a decision to be made lightly. Feeling confused, ambivalent, or even trapped is common. This is part of the process, and it can't be rushed. And if you decide to stay in your marriage, fabulous. Divorce is a private decision that everyone needs to come to on their own. This book doesn't recommend divorce; rather, it aims to guide you through the emotional process of divorce if you've chosen that path.

Although I consider this book to be primarily for women considering or going through divorce, almost every man and woman I know in my age range (early forties) is evaluating their lives. An area they often struggle with the most is the loss of self. "What do I like to do in my free time? Do I even have free time? Is this the career I want? Is this the relationship I want? If I could change anything, what would it be? Have I lost a part of myself? If so, can I get it back?" are questions I hear from married and single people alike. We're asking ourselves these questions at mid-life with the hope that if we made mistakes, we don't continue doing so, and that our remaining years are content ones. Many of us will make the needed changes without getting divorced. But some of us don't feel that is possible. That shouldn't stop us from asking the questions, though. Although reviewing our lives and relationships is difficult, ignoring or denying problems is never a good solution. The problems and unanswered questions don't go away. We just exert a lot of energy hoping they will.

I'm guessing you lost more than your husband in the divorce— you lost part of yourself. And my goal is to help you get that back (not the husband part). I will encourage you to reconnect with parts of your personality that you miss. Your friendships, career, home, parenting, body, sexuality, and finances are examined here to determine what is working for you and what isn't. And if it isn't working, you can explore ways of changing it. If it *is* working, let's celebrate that!

We'll also explore and validate the stages of grief. Staying in one stage of grief is detrimental. Allow yourself to feel all of your feelings, but if you get stuck in any one emotion, seek help. I discuss how to own your part in the divorce without blaming yourself entirely. (Your ex doesn't get all the blame, either.) And you'll learn how to trust, cherish, and focus on yourself, your growth, and your healing instead of focusing on the past or on others. The goal is to make you whole, rather than try to fill a hole with someone or something else.

My divorced friends and I talk most about the changes we're making or would like to make. We don't get together to complain about our exes or our marriages—we get together to exchange ideas and share trials and triumphs. This book offers a similar camaraderie. It does not offer advice on how to "win" your divorce, because I don't view divorce as a battle—there isn't a winner or loser. I will also invite you—repeatedly—to stop thinking about your ex and start thinking about you. One of the benefits of divorce is the opportunity to put your own needs first, perhaps for the first time.

I hope this book can offer camaraderie and guidance in what can be an isolated time in your life. My married friends were very supportive, but they didn't understand firsthand what I was experiencing. Befriending other divorced women was and continues to be my lifeline. If you don't have the energy to do that yet, maybe reading this book can help you feel less alone. Many women have blazed this path before you. Let them help you along the way.

Chapter 1

Congratulations

"CONGRATULATIONS" IS NOT OFTEN THE WORD you expect
to hear when you announce your divorce, but it is the first thing I
say to anyone who shares this news with me. Getting divorced is
difficult and even emotionally devastating at times, but living in
what often precedes it—the "will we make it or not?" state—can be
even worse. For me, it felt akin to perdition—a hell I would never be
released from.

After years of worrying and complaining about my marriage, I
switched to wishing for clarity and decisiveness, rather than for a
better marriage. I no longer wished our problems would go away or
that our passion would be re-ignited. I wished only for a decision
about whether to stay or go. Being stuck in ambiguity was not only
confusing, it was draining the energy I wanted to use for my
children, my writing, and myself. The decision to stay or leave was
made more ominous by my belief that either option would result in
more agony and pain. If I remained in my emotionally distant
marriage, a part of me would surely die. If I left, I would cause harm
to my children and my husband, whom I still cared for immensely.
Although I was often miserable, and so was my husband, I didn't
feel that justified a divorce.

The fourteen years we spent living together included the birth of
two children at home, buying a house, many career changes which
were sometimes followed by returning to school, living two continents
away from each other, the death of Jeremy's mother, and the loss of

several friends through death and estrangement. We grew up together in those fourteen years, and we relied on one another. Jeremy was not only a crucial part of my past, he was a part of me, and I couldn't bear to let that go.

But over the years, I realized our relationship was based on ease and autonomy. We gave each other a lot of freedom, but we didn't have the foundation needed to be able to talk through our differences or the strain of being working parents. We knew how to have fun together, but we didn't know how to be adults together. Eventually, we started ignoring one another, resenting the other one for "having it easier." We forgot what we appreciated about one another.

Jeremy became overwhelmed and depressed once we had children. When I complained that we never spent time together and asked him to make time for a date night—or even better, ask me out on a date, he would say, "Sure." But the date rarely occurred, the time he was going to make for just us to talk as adults rarely happened, and his energy level didn't shift. In six years, we only took one trip (an overnight) without the kids, and I can count the number of dates we had on my hands.

Many working couples have to cope with opposite schedules. This alone is not cause for divorce. But in my marriage, this separation became a choice rather than a necessity. I didn't like this about our relationship, but I also didn't think it was that unusual. And of course, I continued to hang on to the hope that it would change. It wasn't until reading the anthropologist Jules Henry that I started to recognize how not talking, not respecting, and not connecting to my partner could be even more lethal to our marriage than fighting. As he says:

> *Living with a person who neither loves nor respects you, is merely learning how to die, how to walk around in a shell, how to deny how you feel, how to hate without showing it, how to weep without tears, how to declare that the sham you live is the true reality and that it is good.*

Rather than ease and laughter, my marriage became full of stony silences and unmet needs. Our conversations were limited to the kids or the house, and mostly we didn't talk. I didn't feel heard, respected, or validated as a wife, writer, woman, or person. As absurd as it was, I envied women whose husbands were abusive or cheaters. "It's so clear for them that they have to leave and no one would ever fault them for that decision," I confessed to a friend. But my husband was not going to turn into an abuser overnight, and I didn't want him to, so I had to find my own answers.

I gradually began to think that living away from Jeremy would probably be the best thing for me, but I thought it would harm my children, so I stayed. During an individual session with our couple's therapist, she asked me if I wanted my kids to have the same marriage as I had. Without having to think about it, I blurted out, "Hell no." "Then why is it all right for you?" she asked.

In that moment, I realized staying in my unhealthy marriage was providing the guide for my kids to enter a similar relationship. And what kind of role model was I being when I continually told them to follow their dreams, to stand up for themselves, and to express their feelings—yet here I was feeling awful, stuffing the pain and being too afraid to take care of myself by walking away from the marriage? If nothing else, I had to leave my marriage in order to show my children that a different life and a different relationship existed. I hoped that some of Jeremy's energy would return once we separated and that he could devote that energy to being a good father. What I couldn't do for myself, I did for my children. Later that day, I asked Jeremy for a trial separation. He said no and promised to work on our relationship. But I had heard those promises before and this time, I didn't believe them.

"We have to end this while we can do so somewhat peacefully," I pleaded. "We will be connected for the rest of our lives through our kids. Please don't let this get to the point where we hate one another." And with that, he agreed to move out.

Drs. Birnbach and Hyman, experts on working with individuals in troubled relationships, understand the enormity of the decision to divorce. At the same time, they advise being decisive and taking action quickly. "The decision to separate and end your marriage, deciding it's time to go, is a decision that will shape your life, your spouse's, and to a lesser extent, your children's lives, for the rest of all of your lives. Few decisions we can think of rival divorce in its impact. We've spoken to hundreds of people about their marriage and their divorces. ... Almost no one who initiated a divorce said they regretted it. On the contrary, almost everyone regretted waiting so long."

Rarely do people walk away from a separation unscathed: this should not be the goal. Feelings get hurt, arguments ensue, and the relationship needs to be mourned. But getting divorced doesn't mean failure. Staying in a relationship that makes you and your partner or family miserable is failure. Changing your life for the better is brave and worthy of applause. So let me say it again: congratulations on getting a divorce.

If you can make this decision and adhere to it, you and your family can start rebuilding your new life in a healthy, optimistic way rather than continuing to mourn the past and dwell on "what could have been." I took several years to decide to divorce, but once I was done, I was done. Although I grieved heavily once Jeremy moved out, I was also relieved I at least had broken the pattern of trying the same thing over and over again, expecting different results.

Hope is both a positive attribute and a debilitating one. Hoping we can change ourselves is beneficial, but hoping someone else will change can lead to controlling and manipulating behaviors. It also skews our vision of who that person really is, because we're so caught up in who we want them to be. One of the women I talked to, Andrea, a 49-year-old doctor, admitted to doing this. "For twenty years I expected to see my husband walk out the door in a suit and tie, carrying a briefcase. He was a contractor! He had never carried a briefcase and he wasn't going to wear a suit to build houses. When I realized how absurd this vision was, I wondered about all of the other ways I wasn't really seeing him."

My impression of Jeremy was also based primarily on what I hoped he would be, rather than who he truly was. I wanted him to be me. But ironically, I chose him because he *wasn't* me. Where I could be emotional, he was steady. Where I changed my mind frequently and followed whims, he liked stability and remained with jobs, homes, and friends for decades. I married him because he wasn't me, but then I resented him for not being me. And he married me for being me, but then tried to extinguish that in me and make me more like him. We were making each other miserable trying to get each other to conform to our own standards. The healthiest thing we could do was to release one another from this pressure so we could flourish and start being who we wanted to be rather than trying and failing to please the other person. "I'm an apple and you're an orange," I told him. "Apples aren't better than oranges, they're just different and that's all right. We have to let that be okay."

Letting go of the hope that Jeremy would change was heartbreaking. It meant I let go of the hope of having "the happy family." It also meant I stopped focusing on him (what I couldn't change) and instead had to focus on myself and my needs (things I could change). When I truly accepted him for who he was, was when I knew I had to let him go.

It takes courage to make changes in our lives. As therapist Susan Pease Gadoua states in her book *Contemplating Divorce*, "Those who are motivated primarily by avoiding pain are usually fear-based people. ... They are often imprisoned by their fears and will most likely stay small, unhappy, and unfulfilled with the thought that they will remain safe. Action-based people have the opposite view of the world. When they set their sights on a goal, they see what opportunities and benefits might come from moving forward. These people are more willing to take risks and go for what they want. They will also be less likely settle for less than what they believe they deserve."

That's why I congratulate women telling me they're getting divorced. They took a risk and were willing to dive into the unknown, rather than continue with the known, which no longer worked for them or their spouse. They may not know if they're going to sink or swim, and in actuality they'll probably do both, but at least they had the courage to try to make things better for themselves and their family.

It may not feel true in the early stages, but ending your relationship is an opportunity. What that opportunity will be is up to you. It can be as big or as small, as wild or as tame, as you like. But it's yours. By stating, "This no longer works for me," you are standing up for yourself and saying your ideas and needs deserve to be heard. In doing so, you take the first step towards reclaiming your life for yourself. And that deserves a lot of congratulating.

CHAPTER 2

TELLING YOUR CHILDREN

When to Tell Your Children

WHEN YOU TELL YOUR CHILDREN you are separating is as important as *how* you tell them. One of the women I talked to was Joan, a high school teacher who was recently divorced. "One of the biggest mistakes I made was not being firm in my decision to divorce," lamented Joan. "I knew better; I work with kids and know the effect divorce has on them. I never should have vacillated on my decision. I should have waited until I was ready to completely end my marriage before I involved the kids in the transition. The problem was, every time I asked Todd to move out, I was sure I was ready."

After several years of fighting and unmet ultimatums, Joan asked her husband Todd to move out. He resisted and money was of concern, so they compromised on having Todd live in the basement until he could save enough money for his own apartment. Joan and Todd shared the news that they were divorcing with their seven- and eight-year-old children, who seemed to accept the news relatively easily. "Now, I understand why they seemed so nonplussed by the situation," Joan said. "They didn't really believe me. With Todd living in the basement, both of us still sharing parental duties, and all of us eating dinner together several nights a week, what had really changed? In the kids' minds, nothing was different."

After six months, Todd was able to move in with a friend. But after several months of this arrangement, he lost his job again, so asked to move back in with Joan. She agreed to this and soon after, her oldest son started to have behavior problems. "At first I didn't understand what Aiden's anger was truly about. He mostly directed it at himself and would become easily frustrated when he couldn't complete an assignment or task. He'd hurl his homework across the room or break his toy in half and claim, 'I hate this!' Eventually, I realized what he hated was the tension that had returned to the house and the confusion around my marital relationship. Just as he was becoming accustomed to his father living somewhere else and a new visiting schedule, we changed it on him."

Once Joan realized this, she asked Todd to borrow money from his parents so he could find his own place. He dragged his feet in doing so, so she called his parents herself. "I realized if I really was divorcing him, his money problems couldn't continue to be my problems. And when he finally found an apartment, I made sure he agreed to sign a year lease. I wasn't going to make my boys go through any more unnecessary changes."

"Deciding when to tell children can be as difficult a decision as what to tell them," claims JoAnn Pedro-Carroll, Ph.D., author of *Putting Children First*. "One factor to consider is how certain you are about your decision to end your marriage. The process of reaching the decision to divorce is often filled with overwhelming and sometimes conflicting emotions. So it is best to tell the children after your decision to separate is final, rather than while you are in the throes of an argument or still determining how to solve your marital problems."

Although living with disgruntled parents is not ideal for your children, subjecting your children to one parent moving out and back in again a few months later can be equally devastating. Keep all of your back-and-forth decision making to yourself, and don't announce the decision to your children until you are certain. "You're not done until you're done," Beth, a thirty-nine-year-old divorced woman living in Arizona, told me. "Sure, I wish my kids, especially my oldest boy who is rather sensitive, didn't have to witness the arguments my ex and I got into at times. But once I knew I was done, I was done and I never second-guessed myself. I have to give myself credit for that." Once Beth moved out of her house with her boys, she was able to start repairing some of the damage that had occurred in the years prior to the separation.

How to Tell Your Children

Once we knew we were divorcing, Jeremy arranged to temporarily live with a friend and we prepared ourselves to tell the kids. We gathered them into the living room and sat together on the couch. The plan was to share the news as clearly and concisely as possible. Based on the recent sharing of the news of Jeremy's mother passing, I knew my kids could digest only a little bit of information at a time, but they would come to us with questions later. We wanted the kids to be able to have and express their own feelings without being overwhelmed or influenced by our feelings. Knowing that children tend to think their parents' divorce is their fault, we reassured them immediately that it wasn't. We explained that although we had tried for years to resolve our differences, we were no longer able to live with one another without making each other feel bad. We said we wanted and deserved to feel good, not just for ourselves, but so we could be more available to them as well. We explained the visiting schedule and how often they would see their father, and how, although he wouldn't live with us anymore, he would always be their father.

The kids, who were three and six years old at the time, squirmed under the cushions and in general played and wrestled each other during our brief talk. This dismayed Jeremy, but I expected it. Jeremy scolded them for playing, told them to listen because what we said was important, and continued on with his own emotions. I shook my head in warning, but he ignored me and then began to cry. The kids asked him why he was sad and then started crying because he was crying. Although I had hoped the kids could have their own emotions about the divorce, ultimately it was therapeutic for Jeremy and me to sit together on the couch one last time as a family and cry. A few minutes into our "bonding as a family for the last time" tearful moment, our daughter asked, "Can we have mac and cheese tonight?" That ended the divorce talk, for the night at least.

Tanya Valenti, a Washington State-certified child mental health specialist with fourteen years of experience, offers the following tips for how to share the news with your children. "Tell them on a Friday after school so you can both be around all weekend to help them process feelings. Buy or borrow the children's book from the library,

Why Are We Getting Divorced?, *Dinosaur's Divorce*, or *Two Houses* to read out loud. Prepare a 'Children's Bill of Rights' for each of them, in a fancy envelope and decorated paper that states:

> *Both of us love you and always will.*
> *This is not your fault.*
> *This is not your choice, either.*
> *You can feel all your feelings.*
> *You can talk about your feelings.*
> *You can ask for extra hugs.*
> *You can ask questions.*
> *You deserve to have two parents who are happy.*
> *You can ask God for support.*
> *All of us will still be connected to and care about one another.*

She continues with, "You can buy each child a spinning top to represent how they might be feeling topsy-turvy. Add additional time at bedtime to include time to talk and reassure them that the divorce is not their fault and they are loved."

Who Should Tell Them?

Knowing that Jeremy's own parents were divorced and that he harbored more negative feelings about divorce than I did, I did most of the talking. His crying was beneficial for our family, but doing so repeatedly or losing control and making it about him, not the kids, wouldn't have been. As Susan Pease Gadoua advises:

"In a perfect world, you would talk to your children together as a parental unit, remaining as calm as possible when telling them that you're getting a divorce. In situations where one spouse feels extremely emotional, it's fine to wait until things calm down a bit or have the less emotional spouse do most, if not all, the talking. You will want to give the child basic information about what's happening and about how the divorce will impact them. …

Some parents may try to sugarcoat or avoid reality, but in most cases, children see through those tactics. When you tell your children something other than the truth (and this goes for any matter), they learn that their own perceptions are wrong and begin to doubt themselves and their judgments."

What to Tell Them

Gadoua does not condone sharing inappropriate details with your children. Telling them your ex-husband is sleeping with his secretary would obviously not be recommended. Keep the information general and without blame, and keep the focus on informing your children, not belittling or sucker-punching your ex. And this will hold true from this point on. Criticizing your ex in front of your children will not only traumatize them, it may make them resent you later on. When referring to your ex in front of your children, think of him as their father, not your ex. That will take some of the venom out of your voice. It also allows you to start separating yourself from him and letting go. He isn't your husband anymore; he is related to you only through your children.

JoAnne Pedro-Carroll, Ph.D. reiterates Valenti's first tip by stating, "A single fundamental message is the foundation for all of the explanations and discussions that follow: 'Whatever changes take place between Mom and Dad, one thing that will not change is our love for you. We will always be your parents and we will continue to take good care of you. Both of us love you very much, and the kind of love we have for you is the kind that will never end...' Pedro-Carroll, continues, "Children may not always reveal how important your message of enduring love is to them, or how frequently they need to hear it. But telling them again and again and sustaining the message with actions throughout their lives are great sources of comfort and confidence."

My friend Jill, a guidance counselor in Colorado, told me, "My boys are so sick of me prattling on about how it's all right for them to express their feelings about the divorce and how much I love them, but I don't care. I chase them around the house and tell them anyway. Not only do they need to hear it, I need to say it."

The first time my son rolled his eyes at me was when I once again reminded him that the divorce was between his father and me and had nothing to do with him. He laughed, "Of course it doesn't." Yet like Jill, I continued to tell them that their father and I would always be a part of their lives and I was always available to talk about the divorce. This allowed them to feel comfortable to come to me when they needed to, and to be reassured during good times and sad times.

Judge Michele Lowrance says in her book, *The Good Karma Divorce*, "The main complaint I get when I interview children is that no one has explained the divorce to them, or when someone did, the reasons did not sound authentic." My kids' questions about the divorce continued for years after Jeremy and I separated. And every time they asked about it, I did my best to answer their questions with honest information, without making anyone the bad guy. This isn't always easy to do. Sometimes, I probably rambled and wasn't clear, but I talked until they were satisfied with my answer. Over time, my explanations became clearer because *I* was clearer. And my actions probably had more of an impact than any of my explanations. I was happier, clearer, and had more energy for them, which they noticed.

Eventually, my daughter was the one who offered the most succinct explanation. When she was seven years old, she announced one evening, "You and Papa act differently. It seems as if things are hard for him that aren't hard for you."

"That's probably true," I said, and then added, "And that's a big reason why we're not married anymore." My daughter stopped knitting and my son looked up from his book. We all stared at one another for a moment, silently acknowledging that a very confusing issue had just been clarified.

If You're All Right, Chances Are Your Kids Will Be As Well

As described in Susan Gregory Thomas's book *In Spite of Everything*, a large portion of my generation believes that divorce emotionally scars children so we stay in unhappy marriages for our children. Thomas suggests that Generation X suffered greatly from our own parents' divorces, so we are determined to not inflict that damage on our children. This message impeded me in what was already a very difficult and emotionally conflicted time. After doing some research, I learned that studies repeatedly show that children suffer more emotional harm by watching their parents remain in a contentious marriage than by experiencing their divorce. A twelve-year study of over 2,000 divorced families indicated that the key to children's psychological well-being was the level of conflict between their parents when the children were growing up, not whether they remained married or got divorced. When children grew up in divorced families where conflict was minimized, they demonstrated increased emotional maturity a few years after their parents' divorce.[2]

Drs. Birnbach and Hyman support this research by saying, "For adults and children, there is a serious cost to physical and emotional health from the stress of living in an unhappy marriage. The connections between marital distress and children's deteriorating mental and physical health and school performance has been repeatedly demonstrated in numerous studies. The worst solution for everyone is the status quo."

With the fear of ruining my children's lives foremost in my brain, I failed to see that they handled each phase of the divorce phase easily. A year into our separation, the kids continued to seem well-balanced at home, so I began to suspect they kept all of their mourning for school. "He's doing great," the teachers said. "I actually thought the divorce happened years ago, she's so well adjusted."

This still wasn't enough to convince me, so I found a therapist for my son. She fired us a couple of months later, stating, "He's fine, really. But if that changes, you can call me." Though this sounds neurotic now, the therapist's reassurance still wasn't enough for me, so I started eavesdropping on my children. Over and over again, I heard them reference their father's house, or his absence, to their friends in a nonchalant way. Finally, I let my fear and doubt subside and started looking *to my children* for answers about my children. And what I saw were two happy, loving, well-adjusted individuals who were thriving emotionally and scholastically and growing in confidence.

My children have proven to be far more resilient than I gave them credit for. Also true is that my children are more impacted by my actions and mood than my words. I can talk all day long about how it's important to express our feelings and encourage them to talk to me, but if I don't actually make the time to listen to them or show them how to appropriately express their feelings, my words don't have any substance. Since I was able to find healthy ways to cope with my divorce, my kids were able to adjust easily along with me. Chances are your kids will follow your healing path as well.

CHAPTER 3

ESTABLISHING BOUNDARIES WITH YOUR EX

WHEN AND HOW YOU TELL YOUR KIDS you are getting a divorce can set the stage for how they accept and cope with the transition. And although having that conversation is difficult and pivotal, it is only one part of the preliminary process. After that, you start figuring out how to create your new family, one that does not include your ex.

Vast research shows that joint custody is best for children.[3] The only time it isn't best is when the parents aren't healthy, such as when one parent suffers addiction problems. Or when the parental relationship itself is so full of strife and bitterness that parents can't stop fighting in front of the children. Remember, divorce is not what negatively affects children. Living in a household full of tension, bitterness, and resentments is what negatively affects children.

For the purpose of this book, the assumption is that both parties are doing the emotional work they need to do to be the best parents possible. The assumption is also that both parents want to be involved in the children's lives in some way, and that both parents will do their best to be civil to one another while they're around the children.

Stop Viewing Him as Your Husband

"Sure," you say, "but how do you do this while grieving or angry?" The first step is to stop viewing your ex as the person you were

married to, intimate with, and shared a life with. Start viewing him
as a stranger. If you continue to view him as your husband —or even
your ex-husband, which merely means the husband who failed—you
will be stuck in the past. The past didn't work; that's why you're
divorced. And if you don't let go of your hopes that it will work, of
resentment that it didn't, and most of all, of the partner who is no longer
your partner, you won't be able to move forward with your healing.

Divorce expert Robert Emery, Ph.D. says in his book *The Truth
About Children and Divorce,* "When a relationship ends, it is essential
to recognize that the process is like driving on an uphill one-way
street. When the intimate, romantic relationship ends, you cannot
make a u-turn and speed back to friendship or even polite
acquaintanceship. You have to drive all the way back to the bottom
of the hill—and become polite acquaintances—once again.

"All that keeps you and your ex involved now is your joint
enterprise: your children. They are your business and you two are
business partners. Accordingly, your relationship should be businesslike,
which means cooperative, formal, polite, structured, limited, and
somewhat impersonal, or at least a lot less personal than it once was.
This may be a saddening thought for some, a maddening thought for
others, but ultimately it is the best arrangement since it will serve your
children and give each of you the personal distance you need to deal
with your emotions. You are not lovers and you are not yet again friends,
if you ever truly will be. You are parenting partners in a new coparenting
relationship, the terms of which you will ultimately define."

I wish I had read this book—or any divorce book—when I was
separating. I often assumed I knew what was best for me and my kids,
and if I consulted others, it was almost always friends. Although my
friends were brilliant, they were not impartial, nor could they back
up their opinions with years of research.

I did not drive to the bottom of Dr. Emery's hill. I barely moved
my car out of the driveway. One of my main consolations while
contemplating a divorce was, "I don't have to lose Jeremy altogether.
I just don't have to be married to him." I spent fourteen years with
this man; I couldn't fathom removing him from my life entirely.
Even if I wanted to, I knew that wasn't best for the kids, so I tried to
change as little as possible in our relationship.

I thought the physical separation was enough and conveniently ignored the emotional separation. I prided myself that once Jeremy moved out, we stuck with that momentum. He never moved back in because I knew that would confuse the kids, not to mention us. We were also never intimate again. I had the benefit of watching a friend "slip" and have sex with her ex a few times, only to feel remorse—if not outright disgust—the next day. Fourteen years of comfortable intimacy was erased as soon as Jeremy moved out. I only entered his house when invited and always remained in the living room and we no longer touched each other in any way.

It was easy to create a physical distance, but the emotional separation was far more difficult. We called one another with news of our parents or work. We even exchanged dating horror stories. People loved to hear that Jeremy and I were still "friends," and I prided myself on how well we all coped with the divorce. By remaining friends, I thought we were behaving in a mature and healthy way. Being friendly would have accomplished that goal, but remaining confidantes was merely remaining codependent.

Collaborative Is Not the Same as Codependent

When our marriage therapist first suggested Jeremy and I were codependent, I laughed. "We hardly see each other or talk, how could we be codependent?" In my mind, codependent meant being in almost constant contact with one another, rarely attending events without one another, or making decisions without consulting the other. Jeremy and I were the opposite of this. We were autonomous to a fault and led parallel lives. But what I learned was even if I rarely talked to my partner, I could still be codependent. His mood affected mine and vice-versa. I felt paralyzed in my life when he was paralyzed in his. I tried to "help" him by telling him what to do, and his problems became mine. Some emotional enmeshment occurs during all relationships, but not being able to separate yourself from your partner's problems and moods is codependent.

Jeremy and I were codependent, and our society's emphasis on amicable divorce encouraged this codependency. I knew several "separated" couples who still lived together. They claimed the situation was "best for the kids." Magazines and newspapers featured stories of ex-husbands socializing and living with their ex-wives and their new boyfriends. *Redbook's* editor, Stacy Morrison, admitted in her memoir *Falling Apart in One Piece* that she still attended Christmas dinner at her ex-husband's parents' house even when he himself didn't. *The New York Times'* "Modern Love" column ran a piece about a divorced couple who lived together amicably while sharing a bedroom.₄ It appeared that Generation X's response to their own parents' brutal divorces was to try to remain friends with their exes and change as little as possible in order to protect the kids. Although I agree that collaborative divorces are the best route for everyone, I'm afraid many of us are unrealistic about what that really means.

Often, couples will overemphasize the "collaborative" part because they are in denial about being codependent. I told myself that sharing holidays and still remaining friends was best for the kids, but really it delayed our acceptance of the divorce. My therapist constantly asked me, "So what's really changed except you don't live together?" It infuriated me when she asked this, because I wanted to believe everything had changed. I no longer lived with Jeremy and was even dating other men, so I viewed myself as 100% divorced. But every once in a while, a family member would trigger me or something would happen at work and I'd call Jeremy for support. And in that brief moment, all of the changes we made didn't matter, because we were still acting like a couple. And this was not healthy for anyone.

As long as I still relied on Jeremy for anything but being the co-parent of my children, I wasn't really moving on with my life. I dated men but didn't let them into my life and heart in the way they deserved. And Jeremy was not free to move on with creating his own life separate from me because he was still emotionally connected to me. The kids didn't think our marriage was really over; they merely viewed us as living separately. A year after our divorce, my daughter said, "You're divorced? I just thought you didn't live together." Once again, the youngest family member was the one who really saw what was going on.

Disengage From Your Ex

Genevieve Clapp, PhD, author of *Divorce and New Beginnings*, suggests disengaging from the other parent in all areas except parenting, especially in the first year. She suggests following these guidelines: "First, respect one another's privacy. Don't ask about personal matters, especially the other parent's social life, and don't offer personal information about yourself." She also suggests not entering one another's homes unless invited and returning the other parent's key, if you have one.

"Second, do not rely on each other for any non-parenting tasks previously assumed during the marriage. Although these may be a convenience, they come with a price: falling into the old relationship and blurring boundaries. Third, eliminate spontaneous and unnecessary communication with one another."

In order for all of us to really be able to move on with the next phase of our lives, I needed to drive all the way back down the hill and start over. First, I started calling him "your father" rather than "Papa," which kept him connected to me. A more difficult transition was to stop talking to him about my life. I trained myself to call a friend instead. I also started to rely on friends more with parenting issues and concerns. If something happened with the kids, I always informed Jeremy, but I stopped looking to him for parenting comfort. I filled him in on the kids' needs and schedules, but left my life out. Rather than chatting for half an hour when I dropped the kids off, I'd answer with "fine" and "nothing" and race out the door.

This shift did not happen without notice or complaint. My son asked me once, "How come you're grumpy around Papa? He's not grumpy around you."

"Well," I said. "It's difficult to set boundaries with someone when you're not used to it. I'm not married to Papa anymore, so I don't want to act like I used to act with him, but maybe I don't have the new way figured out yet so it seems as if I'm grumpy." He nodded, telling me he understood enough of my explanation, even if I didn't entirely understand it myself.

Change is rarely easy, and usually people resist it. If you are the change agent, as I was, you may sense people resisting you. "Come on," they say directly or indirectly. "Things were fine. Why do you have to ruin things by trying to change them?" Melody Beattie, in her book, *The Language of Letting Go*, says, "When we own our power to take care of ourselves—set a boundary, say no, change an old pattern—we may get flack from some people. That's okay. Let them have their feelings. Let them have their reactions. But continue on your course anyway." She is right. People will have their reactions and resistance to your new boundaries, but you need to make the changes anyway. Because if you don't, you're not really divorced.

I explained my reattempt at getting a divorce to the kids by saying they had two families, one with me and one with their father, but that their father and mother were no longer each other's family. We still spent the kids' birthdays together, but not solely as a "family" as we had done in the past. We both attended the kids' parties, safe with the buffer of six or seven of their screaming friends.

We started spending Christmas apart as well, selling the idea to the kids as, "You get four Christmases this year!" Once again, my daughter was the one to ask the tough but obvious question. "I know you and Papa have your own parents and aren't a family anymore, but you're all still my family, so why can't we all have Christmas together?" My response was, "That is a great question. Unfortunately, I don't think everyone is comfortable with that idea right now. But I can say we'll work on it and maybe someday that will happen." Although I couldn't necessarily see my parents and Jeremy's parents ever sharing a Christmas meal together, I could see a future where Jeremy and his future partner and my partner and I attended events for my kids. But before we could be a blended, happy family, we had to mourn and accept the fact that we were no longer a nuclear family. Being emotionally distant from your ex doesn't need to last a lifetime, but you should at least begin your first year that way.

Avoiding Hostility

In the majority of cases, being too friendly with an ex is not a problem—rather, it's the opposite problem for many couples. If you cannot be in the same room with your ex without fighting, don't be in a room with him. Have the child exchanges occur at school or with a nanny. Do all or most of the communication via email to avoid bickering in front of the kids. Email allows you to have documentation of what you agree to. Even for amicable exes, this is the cleanest way to communicate.

You may not need to keep this routine forever, but don't push yourself to be friendly right away. It's perfectly acceptable for you to be angry, hurt, or sad, so make sure you create time and space to be all of these things. Go out with friends you trust and feel you can talk honestly with, see a therapist, or join a support group. Make time every week to do these things so you don't do them in front of your children. Yes, all emotions are acceptable, but your anger and hurt towards your ex needs to be managed when you're in front of your children. Rage about him all you want in therapy, but never criticize him in front of your children. And try to be civil when you are all together.

In their book, *After Your Divorce*, divorce experts Cynthia MacGregor and Robert Alberti advise being polite with your ex for the sake of your kids, but having clear boundaries as well. "Don't be curt and rude if he's done nothing to deserve this treatment." I'd add to that, nothing *recent* that deserves this treatment. We all know there were problems, or otherwise you'd still be married. But try to let the past be the past, and instead focus on your future, which is co-parenting with this man, not being married to him.

The goal is to eliminate the hostility in the house now that you're separated. Being repeatedly exposed to anger and hostility is what negatively impacts children—not divorce—so remove the anger from your house as much as possible. Complaining about your ex risks making your children feel as if they have to choose one parent over the other. And if you complain about him a lot to them, they may end up choosing him over you. Yes, it may be hard at first, but remember, it does get easier. It takes time to form and understand what your new relationship as co-parents is going to be, but it will happen.

Letting Go of Being CEO

It is difficult enough to manage all of the changes in your own household; trying to manage your ex's household is suicide. It will only cause more stress, strain, and resentment between the two of you. Filling out school forms, making dinner, remembering which day is soccer and which day is karate can be exhausting tasks, but they're not rocket science. Your ex can do all of this, even if he claims otherwise. And the sooner you butt out of his life, the sooner he'll learn how to do these things for himself.

Although Jeremy was a physically present father while we were married, he did rely on me to be the primary decision maker and CEO of our household. In order to share this responsibility, I didn't answer the phone in the first few weekends that he had the kids. I listened to the messages after, to make sure the kids weren't calling, but they rarely called. Nine times out of ten, it was Jeremy calling with a mundane question that I knew he could figure out for himself. And sure enough, within a few weeks he stopped calling me while watching the kids. This not only gave me the "off duty" time I needed, it also allowed Jeremy to become a more competent and confident father.

It may be hard at first, because you are used to and perhaps enjoy being in control. And your ex may not be competent in the beginning. He may forget things at times and won't get the kids to bed at the same time you do and may not feed them the best dinners. But guess what? That's his prerogative. As long as he is not abusive or overly negligent, stay out of his affairs and let him find his own path to fathering.

Have the kids' school send all notices to both households. Notify them of what your kids' schedule is for each household, so they know whom to contact when. Ask for a cubby space for your child's instruments, uniforms, or any other personal items that they bring back and forth to each household. Try to limit the number of items that need to go between houses. That is, unless you enjoy driving to your ex's house in the middle of the night with a trombone or stuffed animal in the seat next to you. All of these steps remove the responsibility from you while your kids are with their father. This approach also prevents you from being the sole information keeper and allows your ex to have a better chance of being in the know and competent. Isn't that what we all hope for?

Paige, like many newly separated women I know, was the ultimate CEO of her household. She earned twice as much money as her ex, was her daughters' soccer coach, and took her kids to (scientifically researched) enrichment activities almost every day. Where Paige was an overachiever, her ex-husband was an underachiever. While married, Paige wrote him notes, called him, and then called him again in order to remind him of something as simple as "pick up the kids" or "buy milk." Her ex grew to depend on this and became increasingly incompetent.

When they separated, Paige tried to maintain this sense of control. She remained the primary caregiver of her girls and limited her ex's visits to a few hours a week—with her on the premises. Even when he offered to take them to their activities, she continued to remind him to do so. Her long-running resentment grew to where she hated being in his presence. Yet she wouldn't let him form his *own* routine with the girls.

Letting Your Ex Fail

Although Paige wanted to blame her ex, I think she was to blame as well. Yes, her ex-husband was unreliable at times, but she had created a life with him in which that was acceptable. He would learn to be more competent only through trial and error. "But he may forget to pick them up from the bus stop," she cried to me. "You're right, he might," I said. "And that will be awful for your girls, and I'm sorry for that. But having them cry or be angry at their dad will be a great lesson for him. And if he truly proves to be incapable of caring for your kids, then you can file for sole custody. But as it is now, you have sole custody of three kids: your daughters and your ex."

It took a couple of years for Paige to stop caring for her ex and reminding him of everything. Unfortunately, several times when she backed off, he forgot, and the girls were waiting at the bus stop or at their after-school activities. This caused a relapse in Paige's ability to let go of control—not to mention a screaming match between her and her ex. Just like when they were married.

As the girls grew into early adolescence, Paige felt more comfortable letting her ex fail. It was still traumatic and embarrassing for the girls to have to ask a friend for a ride home from band practice because their father didn't show. But they at least had the skills to call someone or even walk home on their own. Over time, they expressed disappointment and anger at their father, which Paige knew better than to encourage. (Although she really wanted to.) She didn't necessarily defend their father; she merely remained as neutral as possible.

"It eats me up inside," she confessed. "What is this teaching the girls about men? That they're unreliable and don't do what they say?"

"They may be coming to that conclusion about their father," I said. "But if you provide other strong male role models for them, they won't think that about all men. Ask your brother to pick them up sometimes or a reliable friend's husband. Bring some male friends around every once in a while so they can have a variety of men as role models, not just their father."

When I felt overwhelmed and as if I was "doing it all," I eventually realized I had only myself to blame. "Doing it all" meant trying to be in control, so I delegated some parenting tasks to Jeremy. Whether or not he completed the tasks was not my business. I couldn't remind him or nag him, because then I would not be letting go of control. In order to prevent myself from judging his parenting, I stopped myself from asking the kids about the weekend when I saw them. They filled me in on major events and highs and lows on their own, and I never pressed for more.

Over time, the kids began to reveal disappointments they had in Jeremy or things that he forgot to do. I told them that would make me sad too, and encouraged them to express their disappointment to their father. I tried to do this without belittling Jeremy while still allowing my children to be heard. When my kids asked, "Can you tell Papa to stop doing that?" it broke my heart to have to say, "No, but I can help you tell him how you feel. He'll hear it much better from you."

I couldn't change Jeremy while married to him, so I certainly wasn't going to be able to change him as his ex-wife. I also knew that his forgetfulness and lack of energy was due to his depression, another thing that was out of my control. And although my kids' stability was my number one priority, I had to relinquish that responsibility when they were with their father. The kids wanted to spend time with their father and although I questioned his parenting skills at times, I knew it was important and beneficial for the kids to spend time with him. I couldn't protect their feelings from getting hurt, but I could teach them how to ask for what they need and reassure them that I was available to talk when they were at their dad's. They rarely called me, but seemed to appreciate that the option was always available to them. And I never called them to check in, because that would be trying to assert control over Jeremy's time with them.

When the kids were seven and ten years old, I started to explain depression and its effects to them so they could understand that Jeremy's energy and mood was chemical, not based on anything they had done. I also wanted them to understand there wasn't anything they could do to change their father's depression. My son struggled to accept that. He was convinced that Jeremy would become more present if he asked him to. I repeatedly said, "Everyone, including your dad, wishes that was possible, but sometimes it isn't. But always know that your dad loves you and your sister more than anything."

I won't tell you it is easy to stay out of your ex's affairs. It isn't. And if your kids are being abused or your ex suffers from addiction, take steps toward full custody. But if your kids want to spend time at his house and your ex is loving and somewhat capable— albeit forgetful, overly lenient, or stuck on the couch—you need to let him parent the way he wants. Even when he fails.

If You Trust Your Children, They'll Hopefully Trust You

My friend Rose showed an amazing capacity to let go of control of her ex and his parenting style. Her daughter would often return home from his house unbathed, exhausted, and claiming she was starving because "Dad doesn't eat much, except for chips."

"How are you able to let her go there?" I asked. "Aren't you worried?"

"Of course I am," she replied. "But if I prohibit her from seeing her dad, she'll blame me. She won't understand that I'm worried about her. She'll just think I'm being mean. She idolizes him, and I can't change that. All I can do is hope that one day the shine of him being a musician and 'fun guy' will wear off and she'll see him for who he fully is. Both the good and bad parts."

And sure enough, Rose's hope was fulfilled. After a few years, her daughter started asking her father to cook some of the same meals that she'd had at her mother's house, or her daughter just cooked for herself. His late nights no longer seemed exciting, so she went to bed when she was tired. And eventually, he stopped being the fun parent, and she asked for more time at Rose's house and less time at her father's. She still loved her father, but she no longer viewed him as glamorous. He was just her dad.

Let your kids form their own relationship with their father. As Rose said, getting between your kids and their father is a losing battle. They'll only resent you for it and may even idolize him more because he is the "forbidden" one. Know also that kids often side with the parent they perceive as the weaker parent. If your ex seems weaker, they will help him in ways that they don't offer to you and may seem desperate to get back to his house. Try not to take this personally, and certainly never vent or show your anger about this towards your kids. Trust that it is what it is *for this moment*, but it probably won't remain that way forever.

Your kids are partly yours, which means they are bright and aware enough to see your ex for who he really is, both the good parts and bad parts. If they feel as if they can talk to you without you overreacting or placing your own anger into the situation, they will most likely let you know if anything unsavory or unsafe is occurring. If your kids can trust you to have their best interest at heart, they will hopefully continue to express their feelings and needs about their living situation.

No One Is Perfect, Especially While Divorcing

Your ex will make mistakes and you will as well. Let go of any notions of being the perfect mom and instead strive for being a *present* mom. Being present while eating cereal for dinner with your kids is better than not being present because you're stressed out cooking them Chicken Marsala. Trust me; they'd rather have the cereal. And even more important, they'd rather have you sitting down and eating with them.

Meanwhile, be gentle with yourself and your ex, because you are all going through a huge adjustment. By the time I'd leave the house at 8:00 a.m., I'd have made over thirty decisions and tried to remember at least fifteen things that were supposed to accompany me in the car. I never forgot my kids, but I did forget their coats and permission slips—and my books and notes. Once my kids were six and nine years old, I deemed lunchboxes and coats their responsibility. Phew, two less things to remember!

Getting divorced was a great lesson in letting go of the notion that I had to be perfect and do everything. I used my divorce as my "get out of jail free" card for the first year. I knew things would get dropped during the tumultuous first year, and when they did, I said to myself and others, "I'm in the middle of a divorce. I'm doing the best I can." It wasn't pity I was looking for—it was empathy. Getting divorced is akin to adding another full-time job to your already overfull schedule. It requires a huge learning curve, plus a ton of time filling out paperwork and figuring out logistics. And it's emotionally exhausting. Letting go of your nuclear family and the dream of forever takes its toll, so be kind to yourself. And when you, your ex, or your kids forget something, try to be patient and remember that you are all beginners. Things will get easier and people will adjust, I promise.

CHAPTER 4

CO-PARENTING

THE KEY TO BEING ABLE TO PROGRESS with a healthy parenting plan for your family is being able to take care of your residual issues with your ex. This takes time. Remember you were married for years; it takes years to break patterns and habits to form a new relationship. Also, keep your child's needs in mind, not yours. Creating a parenting plan is not about "winning" or getting back at your ex; it's about making the best decisions for your children.

Be Flexible with Your Parenting Plan

Although many of us are eager to move on and want to remove the stress, grief, and general unpleasantness of the divorce, we can't fast-forward life. You don't know everything you need to know about your future mental state or your kids' needs, so be flexible when making decisions and open to changing your plans if your kids' needs or your needs change. Be patient and forgiving with yourself, and don't try to have all of the answers now. Because whether you admit it or not, you don't know how the next few years will unfold. And the more you think you know, the harder time you're going to have letting things unfold as they should, not as you predicted. Take each day and week as they come. Locking onto plans may result in disappointment.

None of us imagined sitting in a lawyer's office back when we said, "I do." As my friend Marcia frequently said, even five years after her divorce, "This is not what I signed up for." For years, thinking I was in control calmed me, and not knowing my future often caused me anxiety. The divorce caused so many changes in my life that I stopped fighting them and instead felt liberated by being able to say, "I have no idea what I'm doing." While filling out our parenting plan, I laughed at the absurdity of being asked where my kids were going to be on Martin Luther King Day for the next five years. The custody schedule Jeremy and I settled on changed drastically in the mere months between filling out the paperwork and officially filing it with the courthouse. By the time our divorce was finalized, the parenting plan had changed again. We filed our divorce *pro se*, so we never had to check with lawyers, mediators, or attorneys about these changes. We just agreed on matters ourselves. I am grateful for this flexibility, because we could respond to our children's needs immediately, rather than being beholden to a document—or worse, an attorney's fee and schedule.

In contrast, Ellen's time with her son was dictated two years in advance and held to the exact minute, because her ex-husband lived in fear that if she had one hour more than 50% custody of their son, she would ask for extended alimony. Because of her ex-husband's fear and inflexibility, their son's needs were negated and his plea to have certain holidays with his mother couldn't be met. The child's needs were considered when formulating the parenting plan, but ceased to be addressed three years later. This is unfortunate for everyone.

As Dr. Emory says, "You need to bring several crucial elements to your parenting plan: consideration of your children's perspective, a degree of flexibility, and a commitment to developing a reasonable, working, businesslike relationship with your children's other parent." He goes on to suggest that you think of your first parenting plan as a temporary arrangement. After a few months, be open to changing it based on *your children's* needs and continue to evaluate it as your children grow and mature. He also suggests planning in terms of months and years, not minutes and hours, and thinking about your child's needs for the school year, not your work schedule down to the hour. Ellen's plan is the exact opposite of this, focusing on hours and minutes to accommodate the father's fears, not the child's needs; therefore, it doesn't work for Ellen or her son.

When drafting the initial parenting plan, try to curtail your need for certainty in this tumultuous time. I know it's hard—you want at least one thing in your life to be easy and complete. But what children need as toddlers is different from what they need as school-aged children and later, as adolescents. Devise a plan "for now" and agree to reassess it in three or six months.

My kids were only three and six when Jeremy and I separated. Since they were young and used to me being their primary caregiver, we thought they should have more time with me. Jeremy cared for them every other weekend and for a few hours two nights a week. Although this was in the realm of the "recommended" and age-appropriate parenting plan, it didn't work for my children. It focused too much on hours and minutes, which ended up being more disruptive than helpful. After a few of these brief mid-week visits, my son told us it made him miss his father more to see him only for a short period. He had also spent the past four Saturday mornings gazing out the window watching for his father's car, so I knew he needed more time with his father. We changed the parenting plan so the children would be with Jeremy from Saturday evening to Tuesday morning, allowing for uninterrupted time with both parents. We still adhere to this schedule.

Later, I had to admit that my kids' needs were not the only factor I considered when devising the first parenting plan. I was afraid I would miss my kids too much if they were away from me for long periods, and I believed I was the more competent parent, so I thought I should have the kids the majority of the time. Creating a parenting plan to please my ego, abate my fears, and assuage my control issues was not doing best by my children. And doing best by our children is the goal of the parenting plan.

While I was fretting about our new schedule to Marcia, she told me, "I'm going to share a crucial divorced mom's secret with you: You'll grow to appreciate the time you have by yourself. Let them be with their dad." And she was right! I learned to cherish my time away from my kids. Sure, I missed them, but the time away allowed me to be grateful and excited to pick them up on Tuesdays. I took care of myself and my needs while they were away so I could be more attentive to *their* needs when they came back. I got to remember who

I was apart from being a mother. Don't feel guilty about liking your time away from your kids. If anything, feel guilty if you aren't letting them spend time with their father.

Let Your Kids Have a Say

JoAnne Pedro-Carroll, Ph.D. states in her book, *Putting Children First,* "In the best of circumstances, communication about plans and changes is open and abundant and gives children a voice." She states that effective parenting plans alleviate children's fears by answering questions about their anxieties, homes, schedule, money, rules, and communication. When they're creating a parent plan, most parents fixate on the schedule, keeping their own agendas in mind. They often overlook other areas their children might worry about, such as, *Will I still have my own room? Can I call Dad when I'm at Mom's house? Will I still be able to see my friends even when I'm at the other house?*

Carroll lists the following as some of the major areas your parenting plan should address:

- Fears—What will happen to me?

- Homes—Will we have to move? Where will Mom and Dad live? Where will I live? Will I have a room of my own? Will I be separated from my siblings? What will happen to all of my stuff?

- Schedule—When will I spend time with each parent? Will I still be able to see my friends? How will they know where to find me? Will I still be able to play soccer, sing in the chorus, get my driver's license?

- Money—Will there be enough to buy the things I need or want and let me take lessons? Will you be able to pay for my college education?

- Rules—What is expected of me? Are there going to be changes in what I am allowed to do or not do? Will curfew and bedtimes be the same at both homes? Can I take my stuff back and forth between Mom's and Dad's house?

- Communication—Will Mom and Dad talk with each other about me, my grades, what I can do with my friends, how late I can stay out? What will happen if I want to do something and they don't agree? Can I call Dad if I'm with Mom? Can I text Mom if I'm with Dad? And will Mom or Dad be upset if I choose to do that?

Ask your children about their concerns and questions and answer them to your best ability. If you don't have an answer, that's all right: tell them so and reassure them that you are working on it and taking their requests into consideration. Check back with them on any progress you've made about their question. And even if you haven't made progress, remember to update them so they know and trust that you are listening to them. Your toddler's main concern may be how far away her bedroom will be from her parent's room and if she can bring her blankie or favorite stuffed animal back and forth between both houses. My suggestion is to have comfort items at both houses so both houses feel safe and like home to her.

A school-aged child will be more curious about her friends and activities and will need to be reassured that these will remain as constant as possible. Older children may be concerned about money, especially if they hear you worrying about it, and will need to be informed if there will be changes in allowances or expectations of what can be purchased. And all children, no matter their age, need to understand what the rules and expectations are at each house and how and when they will see or talk to their other parent.

Continuity and Simplicity

Jeremy and I operated under the false notion that all childcare should be done in my home (the one the kids were more familiar with) to provide continuity for them. What a horrible idea! I primarily worked from home and was a homebody, yet was exiled from the one place that felt safe to me every other weekend while Jeremy cared for the kids there. I could have lived with this if it benefitted the kids, but they quickly told us that seeing their dad in their "Mom's home" made them sad, because it reminded them of what used to be but was no longer. It also prevented them from feeling at home at their father's house. From that point on, all visits coincided within the parent's own home. After a few mistakes, we also limited the visits from the other parent during these times. Sometimes when we both attended one of their soccer practices or conferences, it resulted in the kids crying. It confused them, made them miss the parent they weren't with, and mourn for their now-broken family. When deciding to do these things, I learned to ask myself and Jeremy: "Are we doing this for ourselves or for our kids?" If it was for us, we tried not to do it. If it was for the kids, I tried to figure out a way to do it where the benefits outweighed their sadness. After the second year, this became less of an issue and we could relax our rule. The children were more accustomed to our divorce, and when it was time to leave an event, we all knew and accepted who was going to which house. I was more secure in my divorced role with Jeremy by then, and we knew how to be friendly, but separate.

I was fortunate to have emotionally intelligent children who could express themselves so clearly, but even when they didn't verbalize their needs, their bodies gave me clear messages. Pay attention to your kids after a visit with their dad. If they say everything is "fine," but present themselves as otherwise, check in with them again. As long as they trust that they can express themselves freely and you will react appropriately, they most likely will (verbally or nonverbally) share what's working and not working.

Continuity is crucial when planning the kids' schedule, as is simplicity. If at all possible, try to have the same schedule every week with as little shuffling as possible. Routine comforts people and unpredictability causes anxiety. Your children are already dealing with one huge change—your divorce—so try to limit the other changes in their lives by offering them as much continuity in their schedule as possible. Some families place a calendar prominently in the kitchen to help everyone understand where they should be and when. One friend created magnets with pictures of herself and her ex on them and placed these magnets on the corresponding custodial days. This allowed her young son, who had no concept of dates yet, to understand when he would be with each parent and for how long.

Mandy, a thirty-eight-year-old divorced mom, had a childcare schedule that changed every week—if not every day. Her three-year-old might switch houses three to four times in a week and then the following month stay with her for ten days straight. Adding to the confusion: a different nanny in each household. The poor boy never knew who was going to pick him up or where he was when he woke up in the middle of the night. No surprise that he started having sleep issues and wetting his bed.

Both Mandy and her ex traveled for work, so for a year, she deemed their erratic schedule as "the way it was." But over time, she was able to free herself from some of her travel responsibilities. And while at home with her son, she established a nighttime routine for him. He still bounced back and forth between the two houses quite a bit, but at least when he was at her house, he knew what to expect. She tried to arrive home at the same time every evening in order to have dinner with her son. Dinner was followed by a bath and story/snuggle time in Mom's bed. This bit of routine and continuity eased her son's sleep issues.

Holidays

Although Jeremy and I were fairly rigid about our weekly parenting schedule, we were very flexible about holidays. For the first two years, we both attended our children's birthday parties, and then on their actual birthday, we had dinner together. The second year we did this was a disaster. It completely disrupted our week's flow—a no-no for our kids. Even worse, the "family" dinner resulted in me crying and the kids being confused. We quickly slipped back to our old patterns of me trying to get Jeremy to talk, my son filling the silence with his own anxiety-produced talking, and my daughter playing quietly by herself. "This is what my life would have been like if I'd remained married," I thought to myself. I couldn't leave the restaurant fast enough.

After that experience, I had to ask myself, "Is it really best for the kids to have a 'family' dinner? Are we still a family?" *No* and *no* were the answers I came up with. It was a good reminder that when we tried to do things our old way, it failed. But when we co-parented while remaining separate, it worked.

These days, most holidays are celebrated with the parent that my kids would already be with on that day. We aren't sticklers for the actual day, even for Christmas and Thanksgiving, so the kids often benefit from several celebrations. Christmas has been celebrated as early as mid-December and as late as mid-January. I've spent Christmas Eve with friends or a partner and Christmas Day alone. When I've missed my kids, I've called them. Or I've just let myself feel sad and then asked myself, "What can I do today that I wouldn't be able to do if they were here?"

Mostly, I can't wait until the holidays over, so I don't have a lot of personal requirements around them. Mainly, we celebrate and plan holidays with the kids' needs in mind, and occasionally the grandparents' requests for visits. If holidays are a big deal for you, ask for what you want in the parenting plan, but be willing to be flexible and consider your children's needs as well.

Emma's children had the opportunity to go to Hawaii with their father one year for Christmas. Although she had adamantly stated she wanted the kids on Christmas for the first three years after the divorce, she relented and let her kids go to Hawaii with their father and his extended family. "I cried so many nights while they were away," she confessed. "Then I'd be mad at my ex for screwing up our marriage in the first place and putting me in this situation. But every time I heard my kids' voices on the phone and heard how much fun they were having, I knew I made the right decision."

Let the holidays be about the kids as much as you can. Don't use holidays as a way to get back at an in-law or your ex. Instead, use them as a way to start building your new family traditions. Again, consistency comforts children (and adults). If the kids always decorate the tree, let them do so, even if you don't want a tree. If a tradition ends up making everyone more sad than glad, talk about it. Ask your kids why they feel sad, and let them talk about their emotions without feeling (too) guilty. Ask them whether they'd like to skip that tradition or alter it to make it feel comforting. And ask them if there's a different way they would like to spend their birthday, Halloween, or Christmas. The holidays don't have to be only a reminder of the past or of what no longer is. They can also be the beginning of new traditions and new ways to celebrate.

Spoiling versus Discipline

If at all possible, try to keep the same chores, rules, and routine at both houses. This can be nearly impossible if one parent is feeling particularly guilty about the divorce or is the one who left. After nineteen years together, Lisa's husband said, "I can't do this," and moved out with little explanation. To make up for the guilt of moving out, his visits with his son were a frenzy of activities and treats to try to make up for all of the hours he wasn't there. He allowed James to watch as much television as he wanted and completely ignored James' bedtime routine. What was fun and exciting in the beginning soon started to overwhelm and tax poor James and he returned to his mother's house tired, cranky, and inconsolable when he didn't get his way.

Before you think you have to start buying your kids' affection in order to keep up with your ex, remember this advice from Cynthia MacGregor and Robert Alberti, authors of *After Your Divorce*: "Fortunately for you, the 'Disneyland/ice cream' ploy works only for a while; after that the kids catch on to the fact that the degree to which they're spoiled is not a measure of how much they are loved. And while it's great (for them!) that Daddy lets them stay up for an hour past their bedtime when they're at his house, they soon recognize that doesn't mean he loves them more than Mom does."

Perhaps you are the one struggling with discipline and boundaries. Maybe your ex was more of a disciplinarian, and you aren't comfortable filling that role. Or, like many parents, you may feel guilty about the changes and havoc your kids have endured because of the divorce, so when you're with them, you just want to have fun and reassure them they are loved. Of course, reassuring them is crucial, but remember: consistency is reassuring, and discipline is a form of love. Letting your kids do whatever they want may please them, but it's not actually taking care of them. Nor is it a healthy way to show them your love.

Dr. Emory states, "As much as children (especially teenagers) may protest otherwise, they also need discipline because limits are comforting. A little freedom from authority can be fun, but as most of us remember from our own youth, too much freedom is frightening. Clear, firm, and reasonable parental discipline marks a boundary of parental love as much as parental authority. Parental authority teaches children how to behave, and it also makes children feel more secure.

"The best style of parenting, authoritative parenting, is to be both loving and firm with discipline. The children of authoritative parents tend to be independent, responsible, and self-confident. This is true whether their parents live together or not."

Dr. Emory cautions that authoritative parents are not authoritarians. Authoritarianism results in children who are well-behaved but less self-assured, because they are rarely allowed to make decisions or have a say in household matters. These children will most likely rebel as adolescents. The key is to be firm but loving, and to treat your kids with respect so they, in return, will treat you the same way.

Shelly, a divorced woman in her fifties, admits that she wasn't able to discipline her girls properly, so eventually she had them live with their father for a couple of years. "It was awful. Here I had three teenage girls, but it was as if they were still toddlers. They didn't cook or clean for themselves. The house was always a disaster. I was working ten-hour days and commuting for another two, so I didn't have any energy left when I came home. I know now what a huge mistake it was to do it all myself, but at the time, it felt easier."

Her girls started staying out late with friends. One of them experimented heavily with drugs, and the other almost failed out of school. Shelly knew she was buried too deeply in her own emotional pain from the divorce and her extremely taxing work schedule to be able to help the girls in the way they needed. With reluctance, she called her ex-husband.

"The girls cried and told me they loved me. They promised to do better, but I knew we were past that point. We were a mess. It broke my heart to do it, but within a few months of living with their dad, their grades improved and they stopped running the streets at night."

Her ex-husband lived in the same town as Shelly, so she was still able to see her girls frequently, but she was no longer their primary care giver. She claims they were distant and angry at first, but eventually the separation improved their relationship. "They respect me now," Shelly says. "Perhaps for the first time in their lives. They always loved me, but why would they respect me? I didn't respect myself."

With her girls at their father's, Shelly was able to devote some time to her own self-care, starting with her health. She had gained a lot of weight and was suffering from dangerously high blood pressure due to stress. Once the girls moved out, she started exercising and changed her diet, and within months she lost thirty pounds. She also began seeing a therapist. While we talked, she picked up a family photo, one where she looked incredibly sad and overweight. "I'm not that person anymore," she said. "I can't even remember who that was."

Mean What You Say

When Jeremy and I first separated, I worked incredibly hard to keep everything the same for the kids. I quickly learned this was impossible and began to let some things go. Firm boundaries are good, but never being flexible isn't. I wasn't a fan of television, video games, or any screen time. I didn't participate in these activities myself and thought it contributed to many emotional and learning problems in kids. We didn't receive cable TV or own any video games, and I used to limit my kids' television viewing to less than an hour a week. And by television, I mean PBS or scholastic videos. We didn't have candy, they always ate balanced meals, and they slept for eleven hours a night. "What a bore," you're thinking—and you're probably right.

With the help of my other divorced friends, I learned to relax on these things a bit. By the time my kids were six and nine, I decided they could watch a real movie occasionally. We still kept movie night limited to Fridays, and I watched the movies with them. A friend bought them *Plants versus Zombies*, and thus the world of video games entered my house. Again, they played this for a moderate amount of time, and it wasn't an extremely violent game, so I was all right with it.

Part of me rejoiced in the new me. It was about time I let some things go. Letting go of rigidness was a good thing, but unfortunately I started letting go out of laziness as well. A more lax bedtime and dessert were fine, but not following through on what I said wasn't. If I wanted my kids to respect me—and I did—I needed to respect myself and I had to mean what I said. When they were toddlers, no meant no. I didn't discuss it. I gave them a few minutes' warning when it was time to leave a location, so when I said, "It's time to go now," we actually left. But during the havoc of the divorce, "no" started to mean "maybe," and "it's time to go" meant "we'll leave as soon as my conversation ends."

My kids caught on to this before I did. "Can we have a treat after dinner?" my son would ask. When I said no, he'd tell his sister, "She may change her mind." And when I'd tell them it was time to leave, they'd say, "We'll put on our coats when we see you walking out the door." Damn them for being so smart.

My son, more so than his sister, needed predictability and boundaries. Unfortunately, my guilt around the divorce made me want to please him and forget his need for consistency. At times, I'd say no to a play date, sensing we were all tired, but then give in once he started begging, telling myself I was just being a curmudgeon. Not only was this not adhering to what I said, it was putting him in charge of the decision-making for our family, which was too much responsibility for a seven-year-old.

Even worse, sometimes I'd negate his decision midway through because I saw the faulty thinking in it. When we decided to get a cat, he wanted two cats and made many logical arguments why this was a good idea. So I agreed to two cats rather than what I thought was best, which was one cat. After a week of the two cats fighting all night and pooping all over the house, I knew I had made the wrong choice. Even worse, it meant I had to renege on my word and tell him we had to give one of the cats back to its owner. Rather than building his confidence and sense of control, which is what I was trying to do, I was actually negating him and making him feel insecure.

I took some time to sort out what was appropriate for a seven-year-old to be responsible for and what wasn't. When it came time for adult decisions that would have an impact on all of us, I made the decision and said it was not open for debate. With his chores, clothes, choices around food, toys, whom to have a play date with, and anything else that affected only him, I let him make the decision and I butted out. Some decisions, though, were open for a family discussion.

When I was clear and firm with my son, he relaxed. Sure, he tried to negotiate and bargain at times, but the clearer I was, the more settled he became. Boundaries made him feel secure. He was old enough to want to push against them, but when I vacillated or was ambiguous, he became anxious, not happy. My clarity, even if it was in saying "no," made him feel secure, and therefore calm.

Your Children's Emotions

Just as your emotions will be erratic at this time, so will your kids' emotions. Some kids know how to discuss their feelings with their parents, but many don't. Even if your children share openly with you, you may also want to seek the help of a trusted friend, child psychologist, or someone neutral that your child will feel safe and comfortable talking to. This isn't to replace you as a trusted person; it's merely an addition.

Dawn Bradley Berry states all children need a safe forum in which they are encouraged to talk about feelings, and that at least some of this healing process needs to be addressed by the parents, even if the child is seeing a therapist. She also states that it is crucial that children are allowed to express their feelings without condemnation or punishment.

One of my main tasks after the divorce was to show the kids that emotions were healthy, and that it was important to express them. For years before the divorce, our house had become the house of stifled emotions—partly to protect the kids, and partly because I didn't want to acknowledge my own feelings about my marriage. Once Jeremy moved out, I realized this certainly hadn't been healthy for me, and it most likely negatively affected my children as well. Both of my kids were extremely emotionally intelligent, but each had a fallback emotion: my daughter's was anger and my son's was sadness. They had difficulty expressing other emotions. My son rarely expressed anger, and my daughter masked her sadness by yelling and stomping. After numerous times of saying, "It's all right to feel your feelings," I realized I had to *show* them how to express their feelings, rather than tell them it was all right to do so.

The first time my daughter said no when I asked her if she needed a hug after a rant, I realized I had gone overboard on concealing my own sadness. I never asked her for a hug when I was sad, and I rarely even cried in front of my kids, so of course she felt as if it wasn't all right to be sad. The next time I felt sad, I told her about it and asked her for a hug. I didn't use her as a therapist. I merely said, "I got my feelings hurt today when a friend canceled a plan. Can I have a hug?" She grinned while opening up her arms. And even better, the next time she had her feelings hurt, she didn't yell and isolate herself. Instead, she asked for a hug.

For years I asked my son if he wanted to throw a pillow or yell when he was clearly angry, but he'd say, "I'm not angry" and retreat into a book. I bought a punching bag and invited my kids to throw rocks with me when I felt angry so they could see how I dealt with my frustration. I'd explain what I was angry about, censoring my admission if it was about their father, and say I needed to "get my growlies out" so I could feel better. Although the kids usually laughed and giggled while punching the bag or hurling the rock against our cement wall, it was still a way to show them how I expressed my anger. Eventually, my son started admitting when he was angry, and found his own ways to "get his growlies out."

From my example, my kids learned that it was all right to express their feelings, and they shouldn't be ashamed of any of their feelings. They understood that all feelings need to be validated, and it's what we do with our feelings that matters. As Dawn Bradley Berry says, "Parents must make it clear that it is all right to feel anger and to express it through acceptable outlets, but that it is never okay to hurt yourself or someone else when you're feeling angry or upset." If my daughter needed to yell and stomp when she was angry, I told her that was fine, but it wasn't all right to yell at us or even be rude to us. And if the yelling continued for a long time, I asked her to do it in her room. (My daughter's voice has been heard three blocks away. You can imagine what this feels like when you're trapped in the same room with her.) When my son routinely claimed to be tired rather than really expressing what was going on, I'd say, "All right, but if you think of something else that's bothering you, will you tell me?" He'd agree and almost always came to me later to share what had happened that was bothering him.

Learning how to express ourselves helped my family with issues beyond the divorce. Dawn Bradley Berry states that divorce "is a golden opportunity to teach children, by example, about healthy ways of relating to themselves and others and weathering the inevitable storms in life." She also states that kids who learn to express and manage their emotions feel a sense of relief, and they gain a sense of self-reliance and self-confidence.

Chapter 5

Making Your Home Your Own

FOR YOUR CHILDREN'S SAKE, you or your partner remaining in the home the kids are used to is ideal. Remember, the fewer transitions they have to face at once, the better. This doesn't mean you have to be shackled with a mortgage or rent that you can't afford, or stuck in a house you have bad feelings about. It just means that when making changes, try to keep your children's needs in mind as well.

Personally, I wanted to remain in my house and Jeremy didn't, so it was an easy solution: I bought him out. "It's always felt like your house more than mine," he said. In the first years of living in our home, I felt as if it were ours, not mine. But over time, I was more interested in the upkeep and remodels than Jeremy was. I financed most of our remodel, worked directly with the contractor, and completed a lot of the work myself. That's how the house became more mine than his. Jeremy had also liked the lack of responsibility that came with renting. When he was ready, he bought his own home, where he was able to have a fresh start.

Some women I've talked to remained in the marital home because their husband moved out and wanted a fresh start. Other husbands kept vacation property or assets in lieu of the marital house. Many couples downsized after separating and moved in with roommates or parents. And a few husbands, like Mark, remained in the marital house while his wife rented her own apartment.

If the House Causes Tension

Mark and Joan worked together while remodeling their house, but unfortunately it strained their relationship even further, and a divorce quickly followed. Mark was more committed to the house than Joan was and enjoyed working on the unfinished projects. In contrast, Joan felt stressed by the unfinished projects and viewed them as the source of most of their arguments. "After living with holes in the wall, tools lying all over the place, and Mark's insistence that he's 'almost done' for two years, I couldn't wait to be rid of the house." Joan wanted to hire a "real contractor" and sell the house, but Mark wanted to keep it. The problem was he couldn't afford the mortgage on his own.

After a year of bickering, they finally settled on Mark renting out part of the home in order to be able to pay the mortgage, leaving Joan free to find a place of her own. "I wanted to rent something as small and simple as possible, but realized that wouldn't be fair for my kids. They were raised with a large backyard in a neighborhood full of kids. I couldn't bring myself to move us into a tiny two-bedroom apartment with no yard even though that's exactly what I wanted." Joan compromised and found, in her same neighborhood, a duplex that shared a yard with two other tenants. "The people upstairs worked a deal with the landlord where they mowed the lawn and took care of the yard for a reduced rent, so I didn't have to worry about it. At the same time, my kids had a yard to play catch and run around on if they wanted."

By moving to a new place with no memories of her ex, Joan was quickly able to make her home her own. Her parents gave her some of their furniture, she bought a few things at consignment shops, and within a month had a new home that felt completely different than the home she shared — and later resented — with her ex.

Many women remain in the house but share the financial responsibility with their ex-husband. I understand this is necessary at times, perhaps to offer the kids some stability. But I highly discourage this solution, especially if money was ever a point of contention in the marriage.

Britt opted for this solution, and it added enormous stress to her life. She had always been very responsible with money, whereas her husband wasn't. While married, they had fought constantly about his lackadaisical attitude about work, income, bills, and his financial irresponsibility. By staying financially hooked together, they then were forced to continue this pattern when divorced. After making her monthly deposit into the mortgage account, Britt would frequently find out her ex-husband's check bounced. This would cause a hostile phone conversation, frustration, and then a phone call to me.

"You will continue to be bound to him in all the wrong ways as long as you are connected financially," I told her. Often, she became angry with me, negated my solutions to untangling their financial dependence, and told me I didn't understand. After a couple of years of this, I suggested selling the house. "But what about the kids? They need this house," she asked.

"Not if it means continuing to listen to their parents fight every month. They've had a few years to adjust. They'll be fine."

Selling her house removed a point of contention that existed for the entire time they were married. It also forced her to let go of her ex and her hostility. His financial struggles no longer remained her problem.

For some women, their lack of earning potential drew ridicule from their husbands, so staying financially connected to their exes allowed them to be continually chastised. Bea was a professional artist and the primary care-taker of her three children while married. According to her ex-husband, who worked in finance, Bea didn't earn "real money" and her job wasn't a "real job." Although both parties agreed that Bea's career would take a step back while the kids were young, the husband became hostile around this and often used "his" money to belittle and control his wife. Him paying her rent every month exposed her to his verbal abuse and control.

If the house was awarded to you in the divorce, or if part of your alimony and child support pays for your rent, then view that as your right. No one, especially your ex-husband, has any right to try to make you feel otherwise. If this continues to be a problem, consider having his payment automatically transferred to the landlord or mortgage company every month to limit the amount of interaction with him. If extreme measures are called for because belittling and tension continues, you may need to consult your lawyer for other options.

Removing the Old

If you remained in the house by choice, make sure to claim it as yours. Obviously, buying the house from him would be a step in that direction, but even if you can't own the home, you can make it artistically and physically feel like yours. If there is furniture or art he left behind that you have always disliked, get rid of it. Even if it means sitting on pillows for a while.

I have had several minimalist phases in the years since my divorce. I actually enjoyed them because it felt Zen-like and peaceful. For close to a year, beanbags served as the only furniture in my den. The kids spent most of the time on the floor anyway, so they didn't mind, and overall the space was fun and playful. A couple of years later, I stripped other rooms of furniture from my marriage. Again, I found the austere nature of the room comforting, and my kids loved the extra room to play.

I preferred living without, over living with belongings I didn't like. When I was ready and could afford it, I bought furniture that suited me and my new life. Consignment shops were my key to making my home feel like mine in a way I could afford. What is old to someone else felt new and fun to me, so I had no qualms about buying gently used furniture.

Painting

Besides removing, buying, or merely rearranging furniture, painting is another way to claim your house as yours. Marcia, my divorce guru, shared another pearl of wisdom with me when she came over one day and found me painting my living room. "Ah, you're in the moving-on phase," she said. "Every divorced woman I know paints her house." She smiled an all-knowing smile and complimented my deep-blue accent color. "It's so you!" Marcia's prophecy ended up being true, and I watched divorced friend after divorced friend paint their houses. A few summers ago, all three of my closest divorced friends were painting their houses at the same time.

The bedroom is usually the first room to be painted, adorned, and altered. For all of us, the bedroom held memories of good times and bad. At some point, it was probably the room where most of the intimacy occurred. But over time, it probably became the place where most of the neglect and resentment occurred. For Donna, the bedroom was the most contentious place in the household. Her husband was addicted to porn, but rarely engaged in sexual activities with her. After years of trying to work on this problem (along with several other problems), she gave Ben a timeline to address his addiction and made an exit strategy for herself if he could not adhere to their agreed plan. He relapsed over and over again, so she asked him to move out, and soon after, she filed for divorce.

It took Donna about a month to settle into a routine with her girls, establish a temporary co-parenting plan to get them through the transition, and adjust her work schedule to meet her family's needs. And then she painted her bedroom. "I can't wait to give it a fresh start, just like I'm getting a fresh start." She painted her bedroom walls eggplant, the ceiling became "perfect day blue," and she rearranged all of her furniture. The corner hosted a reading nook; her bed, adorned with new sheets and comforter, stood regal in the center of the room; and Japanese lanterns hung from the ceiling. The room where she once felt betrayed, frustrated, and ignored was now a place that soothed and nourished her.

In one childless weekend, Donna transformed her bedroom and her home office, which had been buried in Ben's clutter. By removing his clutter and installing shelves, her office once again felt like a place in which she wanted to write and work. With the same zeal, she transformed her garden from an overrun mess to an Eden. A central bed hosted roses, dahlias, peonies, and evergreen shrubs, while surrounding beds held vegetables, herbs, and blueberry bushes. When I visited Donna a couple of months after her divorce, I drove right by her house because I didn't recognize it. It wasn't merely the physical changes she had made—most of which were in the backyard and inside, not visible from the street. But it was also her energetic change to the house that made it unrecognizable. And once I was inside, it felt as if she had installed several skylights. Her once dark and crowded house felt light, airy, and very inviting.

Working on Your House as Therapy

Donna admitted working on her home and yard offered her something to do with all of the frenetic energy stirred up during the divorce. For Marcia, reclaiming her house was a way to unleash herself from her ex's conventionality. Marcia was a glass artist who loved bling. Now that she didn't share her home with a partner who stifled her creative impulses, she hung a neon Thai restaurant sign outside of her glass studio, had a red sparkly faux Christmas tree adorn her living room year round, parked a phone booth in her back yard, festooned her living room in gold, and placed glitz and sparkles in every room of the house. My daughter, a reformed princess but still a lover of anything shiny, adored Marcia's house. Every time we went there, she peered through the window to say, "I think she added something sparkly!" And she was right.

Being a kinesthetic processor, I find it easier to work on emotional issues while doing something repetitive but active, such as walking or painting. I've worked out some of my biggest struggles while pulling dandelions. I've also curtailed loneliness and taken a break from problems and fears by working on my house over my weekends alone. Painting, rearranging furniture, and accomplishing small household projects also offered me a sense of empowerment. Although I was the gardener in the family and the main keeper of our vast beds, I never mowed the lawn. When Jeremy moved out, I considered hiring someone for the task because I had always assumed it was a difficult chore. But one day, I decided to tackle it myself and actually found it very rewarding. "It's as easy as vacuuming, yet way more fun," I told the kids, who were jumping up and down screeching, "Mama's mowing the lawn, Mama's mowing the lawn!" You would think I was a 1950s housewife in an apron for what a big deal we made of this new accomplishment of mine.

During the first holiday season after my divorce, I hosted a dinner party. Unfortunately, my guests failed to realize that I didn't own a garbage disposal. Although I appreciated their help with cleaning up, the leftover pasta, rice, and bits of salmon they cleared from their plates clogged my sink. A male friend offered numerous times to help me, but I insisted on battling the clog myself. When an entire bottle of caustic drain cleaner didn't unclog it, I retrieved a snake from the basement and tried to snake the drain. Every time the friend opened his mouth to offer advice, I silenced him. "Seriously," I scolded, "I need to do this myself. It's a rite of passage for a single mom." I probably wasn't using the 6-foot snake properly, because it did little to unclog the drain. I unraveled a wire coat hanger and jabbed that around the drain until my friend made one too many back-alley abortion job comments. "Wire hangers are not good for much, certainly not unclogging drains," he said.

In the vague recesses of my memory, I remembered the term "P-trap," and that it solved most clogs. I scurried back down to the basement to find a wrench. I loosened what I assumed were the nuts joining what I assumed was the P-trap to the main pipes under the sink. Years of grime had made them slippery, so I struggled to loosen them. I had to ban my friend from the kitchen at this point, because he was dying to give me advice and warnings. Thankfully, I had the foresight to put a bucket under the sink, because when I was finally able to release the P-trap, black, smelly, chunky water poured out of the pipe. Though I was covered in the grime and I'd spent half my evening wrestling with the sink, I was thrilled to have fixed the problem. I bragged about it for weeks after.

Mowing the lawn, fixing a clogged sink, and—months later—an overflowing toilet, all gave me an even greater sense of ownership over my house. Although we hadn't stuck to traditional gender roles, Jeremy had been by far the handier person and the one who fixed most things. By being able to do some of these things myself, I not only felt self-reliant in a way I hadn't before, I felt I truly did own and could care for my house all by myself.

Asking for Help

Equally as important as self-reliance is knowing when to seek help. Asking for help had never been easy for me, and something about being a single mom made me all the more convinced I had to do everything myself. (Which, by the way, is impossible, so don't fall into that trap.) Although it was tempting to call Jeremy, since he was familiar with the house, handy, and wouldn't charge me an exorbitant fee, I resisted doing do. Part of getting divorced is letting go of the good parts of your spouse, not just the bad parts. If I didn't have to deal with his silence anymore, I didn't get to reap the benefits of his handiness either. And if I wanted the house to feel like mine exclusively, I had to stop asking him to be responsible for it. Paying the heater guy two hundred dollars was a clean transaction that would cost me far less in the long run than asking Jeremy to do it for free.

To feel competent, though, you don't necessarily have to leave your own dinner party to snake a drain or read electricity manuals before bed. Take as much responsibility and ownership for house chores as you want. For Joan, she wanted little to no responsibility, and that's why she loved renting. "I don't even try to fix anything," she said. "If it looks or sounds funny, I call the landlord." For me, it helped my confidence to be able to fix things. You may be somewhere in between Joan and me.

Know what you want to do and then find a neighbor or friend to call about areas you don't want to be responsible for. A lesson I learned way too late in life is that people actually don't mind helping. Some of them even enjoy it. I was lucky to have a neighbor in that category. When a wind storm uprooted my lilac tree, he came over to my house with a saw. "Don't spend money on someone to haul it away," he scolded. "I'll just chop it up into pieces and we'll put it in the yard waste week after week." And that's exactly what we did.

Painting sounded like a productive and fulfilling way to spend a weekend, but often by the second day of painting, the slacker in me had wrestled the productive side of me to the floor, and I'd be sick of it. That's when I'd call a friend to help. Even if she only painted half a wall, it was one less half-wall I needed to paint. Plus, her company usually spurred my motivation and energy to keep going, even if only while she was there. A couple of times, I invited several people at the same time and made a social party out of it. No offense to my female friends, but the women usually just drank my wine and chatted while my guy friends painted the tough-to-reach spots on the ceilings and the dreaded sixteen wooden boxes in my picture window.

The more friends and neighbors you can rely on for easy tasks, the more money you'll save. I would never hire a friend as an electrician or contractor, because I prefer those tasks to be clean transactions with professionals, but I learned which friends were able and willing to help with more menial tasks. Calling your ex for help may be a familiar pattern or habit, but it's a pattern you'll need to change now that you're divorced. Because remember, if you want your home to be yours, you have to make it that way. And your home is not his home, so keep his involvement with it as sparse as possible.

Once You Feel Settled, Your Kids Will Too

My kids absolutely love camping because it means sleeping in a 7-foot tent with each other and me. They don't care about furniture, paint colors, or even how much space they have. As Solina Ricci says in *Mom's House, Dad's House*, "Sleeping bags rolled up in a closet can be good beds if these are their own sleeping bags. A house, a yard, and an extra bedroom are just trimmings." Ricci suggests what does matter is that the kids feel as if they have their own space, privacy, and sense of belonging in each house. Whether that is their own room or merely a drawer at one home, it doesn't matter as long as they know it's theirs and that it won't be disturbed while they're at the other house.

Jeremy and I were fortunate to have similar taste in furnishings and ambience, so to the kids, our homes felt similar. We also split our furniture equally, so both houses had furniture that the kids were used to. When new items were purchased, the kids participated in the decision, so they shared some excitement in ownership over the items, especially if the item was for them, such as their beds.

We tried to have comfort items and necessities at both houses. It was difficult to always adhere to this. My daughter has one and only one "Lovey" —a very worn, pink stuffed elephant. I tried to dissuade this for a while by encouraging her to have Loveys at both homes, but she refused. Ricci says, "Whenever possible, honor the children's preferences. If they want to carry their favorite pajamas back and forth, let them. They may change their minds after a week or two and make a switch."

Jeremy's home was new to them, so the kids needed to be familiarized with how his sinks worked versus mine, which locks stuck, how the heat worked, and where everything was stored in the kitchen and in other rooms. Once they were familiar with the home, they were shown the neighborhood. Ricci describes this as "groundwork" and claims it is "the most basic settling in work parent and child must do in a new neighborhood, but it may be the most ignored task of parenting. It takes no more than an hour and should be done by each parent at each home." Groundwork entails walking around the neighborhood, pointing out landmarks, meeting neighbors, stating the boundaries where the child is allowed to walk on their own and which streets they shouldn't cross on their own, and finding fun, kid-friendly places to visit.

The goal is to have everyone in your family feel comfortable and settled in your home. Environment plays a role in this, as everyone needs a space that feels safe and secure. Children can feel that way in rustic settings as long as the parent with them is providing a safe, nurturing environment. Hence, my children's love of tents.

I, however, am not satisfied to live in a tent, so I spent a lot of time and energy making my home feel warm and comfortable. Most of all, I needed it to nurture me, my children, and our new life. This did not require a lot of money, but it did require intention. Rather than thinking you need more space, more furniture, or a "new" anything, ask yourself what it truly is that you need. What feels lacking in your home? What feeling do you want to get when you are there? Inspired? Calm? Nurtured? Relaxed? Perhaps removing items will help you more than adding items. Rearranging furniture can change the entire feeling of a room. Experiment with simple options first. Ideally, creating this new home will be an enjoyable, rewarding task, not one that adds stress and burden to your life.

CHAPTER 6

HEALING IS MESSY, OR
AT LEAST IT SHOULD BE

DURING ONE OF MY MOURNING PERIODS, I decided some service work could help my malaise. An elderly couple who attended the same spiritual practice as I did needed help with transportation while the husband recovered from surgery. I volunteered to be their chauffeur. One bleak, rainy March day, I arrived on their doorstep. Their front yard was covered in whimsical art, classical music reverberated out the windows, and a friendly dog greeted me with a lick. "Hello there," I said to the dog. "I'm so glad I'm here."

The wife opened the door and apologized that they weren't ready yet. I said it was no problem; I had all the time in the world. And for once, that statement didn't depress me. While they shuffled around their house looking for coats, shoes, and purses, the wife told me the story of her husband's recent surgeries. "He almost died during the last one," she said. She stopped her bustling long enough to hold eye contact with me. "I almost lost him, can you believe it? My love of over fifty years. From then on, I slept in his hospital bed with him. I wasn't going to miss out on a minute with him."

You would think this love story would slip me back into my "I'm all alone" depression, but it didn't. Instead, it boosted my spirits because it confirmed that I was right to believe in such a love. It gave me hope that I would find it as well someday.

Healing is a Full-Time Job

But the real gift came from her next sentence: "Healing is a full-time job, dear. Don't ever forget that." I knew she wasn't speaking merely of her husband or herself at that point. She didn't know me or my story, but she was wise enough to sense the sadness that surrounded me. She was also wise enough to know I would survive, once I let healing be a full-time job.

As synchronicity would have it, the couple and I arrived later that morning to our spiritual practice where the message once again was about healing. "Don't ever think taking time to grieve and heal is a self-indulgent act," the Reverend said. "If we are to heal others and the world, we must heal ourselves first. Taking care of ourselves is the least selfish thing we can do. In fact, it's mandatory in order to be of service to others."

While I had been spending plenty of hours grieving in my bed, it was not without guilt. Being self-employed often resembled being unemployed, so plenty of afternoons I crawled into bed to cry or nap because I didn't have clients. And then I'd feel guilty that I wasn't writing, marketing my coaching work more, or designing a class. I felt guilty that I had a flexible schedule while other women I knew didn't. Guilty that I fantasized about hiring a sitter for my kids because pretending to work was easier than pretending to be a highly capable mom. And when the guilt didn't consume me, the self-criticism did. "You're such a baby. All you do is mope. Why don't you get a real job and be useful to society?"

Hearing from wise women I trusted that healing was a full-time job helped shift some of my guilt. I knew they were right, and that I wasn't going to be the mother and friend I wanted to be until I healed. The problem was, I wanted that healing to happen instantly. I didn't want to go through the long dark tunnel called grief; I wanted to quickly and magically pop out on the other side. "All fixed!" I'd cheer as I skipped through a meadow of daisies.

To make matters worse, every time I felt a little bit better, I told myself I was in the meadow, never to return to the dark tunnel EVER AGAIN. And sure enough, a few weeks later, I was suddenly once more run over by the grief truck. "Where did that come from?" I asked again and again.

I may not have seen the grief truck barreling down the highway at me, but in time I recognized other patterns in my life, such as not being called for an interview for jobs I could do with my eyes closed. Sure, unemployment was high, and sure, I hadn't worked for anyone but myself in ten years, but I also believed the lack of responses was a sign that it wasn't the right job or the right time. After a year of not getting called for any interviews, I tried to accept that maybe, just maybe, my job was to grieve, be a present mom, and tend to the clients I had. And that was it. Nothing more.

Although I could convince myself I "needed" every job I applied for, in reality I was getting by with the teaching and coaching jobs I had. The real reason I wanted the jobs was for their distraction benefit. I was sick of myself. Not only did I have too much free time on my hands, but when I actually worked, I helped other people write about their lives, usually delving into deep emotions and their past. Or I wrote about my own life, which was emotionally taxing. "I knew I should have been a bank teller!" I told Jill once again.

"Yeah right, just like I was supposed to be a florist," she laughed. "You'd still be helping people write their stories; you just wouldn't get paid for it."

Jill had taken the prior year off from her job as a guidance counselor at an elementary school. Within a week of not working, kids approached her in the grocery line and at parks telling her their problems. Although she had fantasies about getting back to painting, relaxing, and "just being a mom" for a year, she still helped kids for the entire year. She just didn't get paid for it. "Our jobs aren't just jobs, they're who we are," she said. "That's what makes them so rewarding, but it's also what makes them so hard."

Although I still coveted the income, benefits, and (most of all!) the distraction a "real" job would offer, I knew myself enough to know that distractions don't work for long. The mantra from the children's book *Going on a Bear Hunt* repeated through my brain: "Can't go over it, can't go under it, we'll have to go through it." And in order to go through it, I needed to first accept that I was grieving, and that grief would not resolve overnight. Once I accepted that, I needed to give myself space and time to heal, without judging the process or rushing it or distracting myself from it. I just needed to go into it— all of the way into it.

Tell Your Brain to Be Quiet

Everyone's grief is on its own timeline, and it's not a race. It's also not something that can be taken care of through a few therapy sessions or while on one retreat. I was a slow healer. I knew this about myself, so I tried to honor my own timeline. I watched several friends rush their processes and claim to be all better within months of divorcing. This is impossible. Yes, most of us have seen enough therapists or know enough armchair psychology to know what we're supposed to do in order to heal. But simply knowing what you're supposed to do is not healing; it's intellectualizing it. Healing involves emotions, not the brain. You're only healed when your heart is healed; your brain doesn't get to control it. In fact, your brain needs to get out of the way, because it will judge you and lie to you. Your brain is not always your ally. Sometimes—actually often—you need to tell your brain to be quiet so your heart can take over.

Our brains may at times say, "Quit your crying! You're lucky to be freed from that bad marriage." This may be true, but it doesn't mean we get to skip the grieving phase. Genevieve Clapp, Ph.D. says when a marriage ends, inevitable losses happen, and these losses need to be mourned. In order to heal and move forward with your life, you need to acknowledge and say good-bye to these losses. "Doing so doesn't mean you have to be sad the marriage is over," she explains. "It simply helps you close the door permanently and get on with your life."

In order to quiet your brain and let your emotions take center stage for a while, think of yourself as a little baby or a toddler. You would never tell a baby to "get over it," nor would you tell your toddler she's being irrational. Nor would you lie to a toddler and deny her feelings just because you hoped she would stop crying and get her butt back to work. You need to treat yourself the same way. When it comes to healing from your divorce, you are a baby. It's new and it's raw. You don't know what you're doing, nor should you. You're just a baby. You need time to figure it out.

Talking with my therapist and friends helped me understand that I not only needed to treat myself as if I were a toddler, I needed to go back and reacquaint myself with my toddler self. I would bet a million dollars that your grief is not *only* about your divorce. The divorce may have opened up all of the other big griefs of your life that you haven't healed from. This may sound strange and like a waste of time—if not impossible— but it's important to acknowledge those griefs as well. When I felt overcome with sadness or fear, I imagined my adult self looking for my toddler self. When I reached her, she beamed and we reached our arms out to one another. I folded her into an embrace until I could no longer decipher her body from mine. We had become one. I can't say this vision was the magic antidote every time, but it usually made me feel less alone and more secure. It certainly never made me feel worse.

Grief and Healing Don't Adhere to Your Schedule

In *The Divorce Recovery Sourcebook,* Dawn Bradley Berry states that the two years following a break-up may be the most critical period for emotional healing. "There is work that must be faced and performed during this period if the process of recovery is to be completed successfully." And this two years—not one month or five therapy appointments—is only the first stage of the three stages she claims are necessary for healing.

Tina had a timeline for her divorce. "I'll take six months to grieve and normalize things for my kids, then I'll enter a long-term relationship with a man who will understand and desire children and be able to meld into my family and my lifestyle," she told me.

I was speechless for several moments after hearing this. "Wow," I eventually said. "You have it all figured out. All I could do was get through each day as it came."

In truth, Tina wasn't able to follow her plan. Emotions don't care about timelines; they are unruly buggers who come and go as they please. And meeting a person, falling in love, and establishing a new family—all accomplished by a random calendar date? Good luck with that. If it does happen that way, I'm guessing you will have chosen your partner erratically, and you may spend months convincing yourself he's the right one—until your house of cards crumbles. Again.

Jill and I went through our divorces at the same time, but were rarely, if ever, experiencing the same emotions or behaviors at the same time. She started the process at least a year before I did, but remained in the bargaining phase longer than I did. Both of our stages and emotions looked like roller coasters, but we were riding different rides. I'd call her in tears, feeling despondent about my loss and worried about my kids, and she'd say, "But it's the right thing to do. You know it's best for all of you." She'd tell me about her night out with her girlfriends, giddy with her new freedom, and remind me of the positive outcomes of our divorces. Three weeks later, she'd call me, missing her ex, and I'd remind her of the not-so-pleasant times with him.

Our different reactions were a reassuring reminder about the impermanence of each phase and mood. "People progress through the necessary stages of healing at different paces with different emotions surfacing at different times, and the process should not be rushed. It takes time to grieve the loss of the good times even in a difficult marriage, the unfulfilled dreams, and the unmet expectations," explains Dawn Bradley Berry in *The Divorce Recovery Sourcebook*.

If nothing else, I hope you learned from your marriage that you can't control your ex or your relationships. So please, don't try to control your healing process. It's a losing battle. Just when you think you are over your grief is often when you find yourself sobbing in your bed. Triggers occur when you don't expect them. Emotions are messy, and unfortunately, there's nothing we can do about that. In fact, the best thing to do is let them be messy and debilitating, trusting that those feelings will pass and eventually you'll get to the other side and feel joy and hope again.

Divorce Affects Both Partners, Even the One Who Left

People spend lots of time trying to assess who wanted out of the marriage first and who left whom. They pity the person who was left and make the leaver a villain. They also assume the one being left is going to have a harder time recovering, and the leaver is probably already off enjoying a new life. Although some of this holds true for some people, no one escapes a divorce or break-up unscathed. When a loving relationship ends, everyone hurts and no one wins. It may be more complex and difficult to be the one who was betrayed or left, but once love is involved, no one remains unaffected.

I dated a man who spent an inordinate amount of time trying to make sure he would always be the person who left the relationship. Love was terrifying for him, so his primary goal in relationships was to avoid being hurt. He literally trembled when he felt love for me. "No one gets out of this one alive, huh?" he'd ask. I'd shake my head and smile. Not because I'm sadistic, but because I'm someone who views love as rewarding and beautiful. Sure, love can be messy, but to do without love is not conceivable for me. He viewed love as a dark dungeon filled with barbed wire. Needless to say, when he left me, we both ended up on the barbed wire. But he was able to console himself that he got out before it was "true carnage."

John W. James and Russell Friedman, founders of the Grief Institute and authors of *The Grief Recovery Handbook*, believe everyone involved in a divorce is a griever. "We also know that the primary unresolved issue is grief. Incomplete grief over a former spouse will dictate fearful choices. Incomplete grief will create hypervigilant self-protection from further emotional pain. Sadly, this excess of caution limits the ability to be open, trusting, and loving, dooming the next relationship to failure."

I know you don't want to become the person James and Friedman describe above (trust me, I dated him), so complete your grief cycle. But how, you say? According to the Kübler-Ross models, the stages of grief over losing a loved one are Denial, Anger, Bargaining, Depression, and Acceptance. Many experts agree the stages for grieving a divorce are similar, as they should be, because divorce is also a death. Erica Manfred, in her book *He's History, You're Not*, is so bold as to say, "Some therapists think it's worse than the death of a spouse...Unlike grief after the death of a spouse, there are no acceptable ways to grieve the end of a marriage. You can't sit shiva or hold a wake, no one will bring casseroles..., and—worst of all—no one who hasn't been there will really understand what you're going through."

Similarly to grieving any death, you must go through the four phases of denial, anger, bargaining, and depression before you get to the glorious meadow, which is acceptance.

Denial

After our last marriage counseling session, where we told our therapist we were getting divorced, Jeremy and I sat in my car for over an hour crying. "It's really over?" we asked one another, and then cried some more when the other one nodded. I can't remember ever feeling worse. We repeated this scene a few times, but even with this sense of closure and the year of couple's therapy leading up to it, I still found myself gasping when the sudden thought, "I'm divorced" popped into my head. I hadn't necessarily been telling myself I was still married, but I wasn't fully on the other side to acknowledge I was divorced. I was in the in-between place otherwise known as denial.

My friend Jill is a guidance counselor for the school district so part of her job is talking with families as they divorce. Time and time again, one of the parents would ask for a subsequent meeting years after the divorce. During this meeting, the parent would mention they are divorced, as if this was news to Jill. "Yes, I know. I met with you, your ex, and your daughter countless times during your divorce, remember?" Jill would reply. The parent would then look at Jill with a blank stare and spend the rest of the session processing the divorce. As I said, you may know things to be true, but that doesn't mean you've accepted them.

DENIAL AS A PROTECTOR

Although denial often keeps us in bad situations longer than we should be, it isn't doing so solely in a tormenting bully kind of way. It's also protecting us. The mind and self can only absorb so much change, fear, and sadness at once, so denial becomes a buffer. I view denial as a large tree with many branches to help break our fall. "Maybe we'll work things out," is one branch. Another branch is, "When he gets his new job, it will be easier." The tree offers us as many branches as we need to buffer our fall. To fall straight from the top of the tree to the unyielding cement below would be too devastating, so use the branches when you need to. But know that eventually, you need to hit the ground below. Otherwise, you'll be stuck in limbo forever. And the sooner you reach the ground, the sooner you can pick yourself back up again.

Melody Beattie, author of *The Language of Letting Go,* says we become experts at using denial to make reality more tolerable. "We have learned well how to stop the pain caused by reality—not by changing our circumstances, but by pretending our circumstances are something other than what they are. Do not be too hard on yourself. While one part of you was busy creating a fantasy-reality, the other part went to work on accepting the truth. Now, it is time to find courage. Face the truth. Let it sink gently in. When we can do that, we will be moved forward."

People often mistakenly think they are fine and done with their grieving process, when in actuality, they haven't even begun. Denial—or sometimes shock—gives us the false impression of feeling all right even when we aren't. Opal's husband of seventeen years came home one day and said, "I'm done." He refused to go to couple's therapy, denied the involvement of another woman (a lie), and claimed Opal was too difficult to live with. Within two months of his departure, Opal started dating, claiming, "I'm fine." As a child, she had been the caretaker of a severely ill sister and an alcoholic mother. Never in her forty-eight years of life had it been all right for Opal to not be "fine." She treated the betrayal of her husband just as she had treated every other problem in her life: she ignored it and carried on.

By not grieving or even shedding a tear, Opal was able to convince herself that she was strong and capable. She went as far as telling herself that she was glad he left and that it didn't bother her. By shutting out her sadness, she started to shut out all of her other emotions as well and started to "feel flat." An overachiever, she assumed taking on more work responsibilities and committing herself to more engagements was the key to feeling good again. This provided a distraction for a while, but it also stalled her healing progress. As Melody Beattie says, "A block to joy and love can be unresolved sadness from the past. ... We denied that it hurt because we didn't want to feel the pain. Unfinished business doesn't go away. It keeps repeating itself, until it gets our attention, until we feel it, deal with it, and heal."

Opal's dating spree was a way she could tell herself she was healed and ready to move on. Unfortunately, rather than healing in a trusting relationship, she continually chose unavailable men who left within months. Again, she didn't mourn these losses, but merely moved on. Eventually, she dated a man who was relatively available, but once they became intimate, she broke it off. Since she hadn't addressed any of her past hurts and abandonments, she was unable to open herself to another person. And this inability made *her* emotionally unavailable. Not only to men, but to her friends and family as well.

In Opal's case, denial offered her a buffer before facing over forty years of neglect and abandonment. If she acknowledged one layer of abandonment—the recent one by her husband—it could reveal all the others. Although this type of issue needs to be addressed at some point, it's best done slowly and with the help of a trained therapist. Try to remember that denial is sometimes protecting you, even if it is messing up your life. It's the overbearing sister who needs to be told at some point, "Thanks for helping me, but I've got it from here."

Anger

IT, YOU, AND HIM

All emotions are messy, but I found denial neat and orderly compared to the unruly rebel anger. I was not familiar with anger and felt surprised every time I felt the urge to slam a door or yell. Even more confusing: I didn't understand who or what I was mad at, so why was I slamming doors? A friend helped me realize I was angry that my marriage had failed. It's confusing to feel angry at a circumstance, because you can't pick a fight with a circumstance. Circumstances don't have a name to yell or a face to throw a dart at, and they rarely fight back. It's also confusing to be angry about a circumstance that, in the end, you initiated yourself.

I continued to bump up against society's norms and my norms, which told me I had failed. Even though I knew otherwise, I had to fight these feelings. I don't like to fail. I like to do things well and be instantly proficient. Failing at my marriage was intolerable, more so when I felt I failed at being a single mom as well. The learning curve on being a single parent was big, and this pissed me off.

After slamming doors, crying to friends, and taking up a lot of strenuous exercise to help release my anger about my divorce, it was time to look at *my* part of the end of my marriage. Part of the healing from my divorce was addressing my negative behaviors and characteristics so I wouldn't repeat them. Again, not being able to rid myself (instantly) of these negative characteristics pissed me off. When I examined why I felt overwhelmed and as if I was doing everything I had to admit it was due to my control issues. Damn it! That unruly bugger again! Obviously, trying to control my control issues wasn't going to work, so I had to find new coping mechanisms. This also pissed me off.

The anger phase was terrifying at times because it physically overwhelmed me. I had usually stuffed my anger so it manifested itself as depression. Learning to direct that anger outward rather than inward was a huge relief, but it was also unfamiliar and frightening. Rather than being exhausted—a result of being depressed—instead I had an endless amount of energy. But it wasn't constructive energy. It was frenetic and disruptive.

Brain chemistry explains that the primary rage system is closely linked to centers in the prefrontal cortex that anticipate rewards. The common response to unfulfilled expectations is known as frustration-aggression. In short, when people and other animals begin to realize that an expected reward is in jeopardy—or worse, unattainable—these centers in the prefrontal cortex trigger fury. This can trigger excessive energy and obsessive thinking.[6]

The reward I obsessed about was feeling all better or at least somewhat better, and when that didn't happen, I was overcome with excess energy. Some of this could be channeled toward work, but most of it needed to be released physically. I took up hiking and yoga, and I increased my daily exercise. When a four-hour hike wasn't an option, I purposefully hurled plates, tiles, and rocks against a cement wall. The kids wanted in on the fun, so we bought a bunch of cheap plates at Value Village to smash. I let them hurl the plates against the wall in our backyard or handed them safety goggles and hammers and let them smash the plates that way. They loved it, especially my daughter. We decorated our mailbox in a mosaic pattern with some of the remnants. This provided a reward, but not the ultimate reward of being all better that I was seeking. But at least it got me a step closer.

Next, and perhaps the most difficult phase of anger, was when I had to look at Jeremy's part of the failed marriage. If I didn't look at his part, I would continue to have the divorce-that-wasn't-really-a-divorce because I wouldn't be emotionally divorced from him. But being angry at Jeremy felt like kicking a puppy. When I explained this to my therapist, she said, "That's harming you as well as Jeremy. He doesn't want to be pitied like a puppy; give him the decency to be treated like a man." If I continued to protect Jeremy not only from my anger, but from any news that could hurt him (such as going on a vacation with a boyfriend), we would never truly move on and recover. And that would be worse than kicking a puppy.

I finally let my anger towards Jeremy out with my therapist and a few friends. "Sure, he's a very loving father, but I have to do everything. I sign them up for swim lessons, I stress about what school they should go to, I interview shrinks for them. I take charge of their emotional, educational, and spiritual development. And sometimes I even have to be the one to kick the damn soccer ball with them in the rain!" And thus, the dam was broken and it was now all right to kick the puppy.

Obviously, expressing your anger about your ex in front of the kids is not acceptable. Nor do you want to assign all of the blame for the failed marriage to him. But seeing your part in the divorce as well as his is a step towards accepting that the marriage is over. And that step must be taken to move on in a healthy way.

ANGER IS ALL RIGHT, BITTER RESENTMENT ISN'T

Women tend to avoid feeling anger because it frightens them. Our society unfairly and unfortunately does not accept angry women and instead denounces us as hysterical or a bitch if we express true anger. Thus many women manage to stifle their rage until it calcifies as bitter resentment. Being resentful keeps us from moving on, and as Erica Manfred says in her book *He's History, You're Not*, "Moving on has to be your ultimate goal."

Resentment wraps you in an impenetrable bubble. Don't let your anger build to that point. Talk about your anger with others, express it, and feel it, but then try to move on from it. For me, that meant crying. Once I had raged, ran, and hurled plates, I usually wept.

Crying released the anger and allowed my body and mind to finally feel at ease. Sad, but at ease. And from there, I could move forward without being fueled by anger.

Six years after her divorce, Kate claimed getting divorced was the best thing she's ever done. (In fact, she claimed that just *four days* after her divorce.) Yet almost every conversation with her still involved a reference to her ex-husband. At times she ranted; at other times, she seemed to pity him. The emotions themselves weren't troublesome; the problem was that he still occupied so much of her mental space. He had moved to another city, remarried, and even had two new children with his new wife. Whereas Kate had not gone on a single date.

I'm not saying remarrying is the only way to move on, but I do think thirty-eight is too soon to resign yourself to being a spinster. Kate was young, attractive, extremely bright, and successful with her career. She's an incredibly funny and compassionate woman. Men were drawn to her, but she kept herself protected by her anger and wouldn't as much as engage in conversation with guys she didn't know. No man could access her because she had not let go of her ex-husband. She was still married—but without any of the benefits.

She claimed her life was much fuller now that she was free to do as she pleased, which was true on some levels. But it seemed to me that almost all of Kate's drive came from doing things to prove her ex-husband wrong, rather than doing things that pleased her. After an accomplishment or trip she usually said, "He would never have appreciated that" or "I never could have done this if I were still married."

One of my kids' favorite books, *Zen Shorts*, beautifully narrates the harm in not letting go of anger. An elder monk carried a female across a puddle so she wouldn't get wet and dirty. Rather than thanking him for being kind, she shoved him out of the way and walked away. A young monk was upset about this and told the older monk he thought she was rude and selfish. "I set the woman down hours ago," the older monk replied. "Why are you still carrying her?" It was time for Kate to put her ex-husband down. He was too heavy to carry, and her resentments towards him hurt only her. Meanwhile, he was off living a full, happy life.

Express your anger about your ex, your failed marriage, or anything else that is bothering you before it builds to resentment. Resentments come from anger that hasn't been released, which keeps you connected to your ex in a way that is not healthy or useful. You can end up not moving on because your anger at him keeps you stuck in the past. The false assumption is that you're punishing him, but in actuality, you're hurting yourself and your kids. The resentment can keep you isolated and prevent you from truly living the life you want. You can end up blocked from being connected to yourself and others because you're overshadowed by your ex. And it hurts your kids to live with an angry, resentful mom who is not moving on with her hopes and wishes for a better life.

WAYS TO EXPRESS ANGER

All feelings are valid, so you have to let yourself feel all of them. Where and how you express your anger is tricky, because you don't want to frighten your children. Being angry in front of your children is acceptable, as long as you take the time to explain to them that you aren't mad at them; you are merely frustrated about a situation. Screaming at your children because you're angry about your divorce is not acceptable. Even if you're angry at them, screaming is never a good idea. And if you find yourself doing so or wanting to, call a friend. Or even better, a therapist. Talk to people, join a gym, take up kickboxing or tennis; do whatever it takes to provide an outlet for your anger.

Even if you don't think you're angry, you probably are, and your anger will find inappropriate ways to reveal itself if you don't address it first. One day you'll find yourself screaming at traffic, whereas the day before, your drive was calm. Or you'll have insomnia, feel overly frustrated, or find less patience for your kids and your job. These are all signs that anger has built and is now bubbling over and making a mess. Find appropriate outlets for your anger and release it in a healthy way, not a destructive way.

ANGER, JUST LIKE GRIEF, CAN BE A REPEAT VISITOR

For those of you who've expressed your anger, mastered the art of kickboxing, and are now "moving on" with your life, I say "Congratulations!" And then I cautiously add, "Be careful: another round of throwing plates may come back. But don't worry! You know how to deal with it now." As you know by now, emotions are unruly bastards, and they do not adhere to our desired schedule.

Another round of anger emerged when I started dating. Ironically, it wasn't when the relationship failed that I raged. Instead, it was when it *worked*. Having needs met that I thought would never be met because I was told so made me incredibly grateful. And then angry. I had been deemed too intense and sensitive my whole life. I'd felt shame about this, and I often didn't reveal my true self to others, due to fear of being rejected or ridiculed. But post-divorce, I met a lot of people who valued my insights and my ability to discuss my emotions. Being met in this way, especially by men I dated, shifted my lifelong perception of being "too needy." And that's when the anger came back.

"It's not that complicated," I said to Jill in yet another phone call. "It's called 'pay attention to us and listen to us.' It's so basic, yet we were made to feel terrible about asking for it." Jill had also felt as if she was too needy, and she was repairing that damage by being in a relationship with—you guessed it—a psychologist. Ironically, once Jill and I felt heard in our relationships, we stopped needing to process every thought and feeling. "Oh honey," I said on one of my trips with a boyfriend, "let's just go to the beach and not think. All that stuff about where our lives are going or not going will still be there tomorrow."

"Did Corbin Lewars just refuse an opportunity to be introspective?" he said, laughing.

"I'm on vacation! Don't worry; I'll introspect again once we're back in Seattle."

And of course, witnessing your ex remarry or start a relationship may trigger your anger. We all hope to be the one who moves on first, but remember, we're not in charge of everything. If running into your ex and his new wife pisses you off, let it piss you off. Get out the boxing gloves (at home, not on him), call a friend, run a mile, or do whatever you need to do to express that rage. And then remind yourself that you are healing and moving on as well. You may not being doing it at the pace you hoped for or at his pace, but you are doing so at the pace that is best for you.

Bargaining

I spent years prior to my final decision to divorce bargaining with myself. I constantly told myself, "If he'll just agree to..." and "It will get better when..." One of the most meaningful evenings during these times was a night spent with my friends Deb and Lori. Deb said, "Corbin, for years you have been coming over here upset about your marriage. What are you going to do about it?" Seeing it stated in such a neutral way and by a trusted, long-time, benevolent friend, I finally heard it and took it to heart. Up until that point, I had been too caught up in bargaining to be able to see the marriage for what it was, not what I hoped it would be. To hear a woman who knew me well point out that I'd been sitting on her couch crying for years about the same exact problems told me I needed to do something different.

So I took my bargaining to Jeremy and asked him to do something about his depression. I don't actually recommend this strategy, because bargaining often leads to ultimatums. As you'll learn later in this book, ultimatums rarely get you what you want. All in all, I can't say bargaining worked out too well for me, but it did accomplish something very important: it got me divorced. Once I realized that's what I was doing (thank you Deb), I realized that bargaining was all that was holding my marriage together. A marriage can't survive on "if only" and "when he ____"; it needs a much firmer foundation. Once I let go of bargaining, I could let go of Jeremy.

Some of us make the decision to divorce, but still hold on to the "once he does ____, we'll get back together" notion. We don't always do this consciously; it's a sneaky part of the bargaining phase. If you rushed into the decision to divorce, the bargaining phase may last longer than you like. As I said, you're not done until you're done. Take some time for yourself and don't judge your mixed feelings. All of your feelings and stages are valid. You'll eventually be ready to let your ex go completely, but until that happens, bargaining and other phases can offer a reprieve from the grief. As Kübler -Ross and Kessler describe in *On Grief and Grieving*, "Bargaining can help be an important reprieve from pain that occupies one's grief. In other cases, bargaining can help our mind move from one state of loss to another. It can be a way station that gives our psyche the time it needs to adjust. Bargaining may fill the gaps that our strong emotions generally dominate, which often keep suffering at a distance."

Depression

Adjusting to being a single mom was difficult. I didn't know how to ask for help. I assumed I had to do everything myself, and I was often overwhelmed, frustrated, and exhausted. I was worried about money, about how I was going to balance work and be a mom, and a slew of other things, which started keeping me up at night. My lack of sleep propelled me right into the old familiar pattern of being irritated and depressed.

"This again?" I complained. "I had enough of this while contemplating divorce. I thought it would be better now." And it was better at times, but often it wasn't. I was afraid I had exhausted my friends with all of my pre-divorce crying and whining, so I started keeping to myself. I felt as if I had to put on a smile and be interesting, engaging, and fun with others. When I didn't think I could be cheery, I stayed home. This was a mistake and often only caused me to feel lonelier and more depressed.

REACH OUT TO FRIENDS

Eventually, I realized isolating myself wasn't helping me, so I reached out to more people. Besides Jill, whom I relied on heavily, my friend Cedar had also split from her partner of twelve years. I viewed her as a sister in many ways, and I trusted her as someone who had thrived after a break-up and who would honor my feelings without judging me. And when I felt as if I was depending on Cedar too much, I showed up on my friend Erika's doorstep. By spreading my sadness around to a few friends, I could reassure myself that I wasn't taxing any one friend too much.

Even if you think you can bear being out for only an hour, do it. At a minimum, it will be an hour break from yourself. At best, it will be a fun and interesting evening. I reached out to friends a lot while depressed, but occasionally had a day in which all I could do was make it through work, pick up the kids, and then crawl into bed when they did. One day of this was fine. If it persisted for two or three days, I made myself call my therapist.

HONOR THE SEVERITY AND DURATION OF YOUR HEALING PROCESS

The problem with depression is it disables you from being able to do what you need. Getting exercise, getting out of the house for a while, or calling a friend can usually help alleviate some of the depression, but when you're depressed, these sound like Herculean tasks. My friend Diane calls depression "wading through mud" or "walking around with 1000-pound weights on your ankles." The excessive energy I felt with anger was no picnic, but at least I was usually productive during those times, and I knew the anger was usually fleeting. Denial could last forever, but who cares? You're in denial, so you think you're doing fine. The problem with the depressed stage—which I found to be the worst phase—was that I was always sure it would last a long time. And frankly, even five minutes spent wading through mud feels like eternity.

I learned that the more I wished it would go away, the longer it stayed. Instead, I learned to say, "Oh, hello there burdensome friend. I see you're back," when I started to feel the weights on my feet return. I didn't start wishing for it to become a permanent houseguest, but I didn't deny its existence or try to make it go away instantly, either. Because just like all the other phases, the more I tried to control depression, the more debilitating it became. Merely acknowledging it rather than trying to understand it, explain it, rationalize it, or kick it out actually helped it leave quickly on its own. Maybe after an hour or maybe after a day, it ceased to matter, because I wasn't battling with it.

For me, depression caused me to feel flat about life, or as if I wanted to escape to a warm island and not think about my problems. I recall saying I wished someone would hit me over the head with a baseball bat and "wake me up when it's over," but that was about as bad as I ever felt. If your depression is more severe than this, know that you are not alone, but seek help quickly. According to Dawn Bradley Berry, a very high percentage of women experience a severe depression that interferes with their day-to-day functioning. They can't get out of bed for days, or they feel suicidal or as if they are going to die from their grief. This level of depression needs to be treated but never judged. Judging your depression only makes it worse, so seek help and start talking to someone. And remember, you're not the only one who has ever felt that way.

According to psychologist Genevieve Clapp, there could be a positive aspect to the severity of your feelings. In her book, *Divorce and New Beginnings*, Clapp states that her studies revealed that the people who were the most upset after their breakup healed the fastest and most completely, probably because they let themselves feel everything fully and sought help when they needed it.

According to Erica Manfred, the feeling of thinking you'll die after a divorce may not be due to mere sadness or heartbreak, but to an actual biological trigger. She claims it stems back to our days as tribal women when our primal role was to be keep the fire going and keep the children nearby in the cave so they could be safe. Learning from the teacher Patricia Wall, Manfred extrapolates that if we didn't do these tasks successfully, we not only failed, but we or our children may have died. Twenty-first century women have a biological connection to their ancestors, sharing the perception that their role is to keep their families safe and whole. When they divorce, they feel as if they failed, and therefore as if they may die. Manfred says, "When my husband left, I actually felt as though I wasn't going to survive; the separation might kill me. …. We women take responsibility for marriage, for keeping the tribe together, and if it falls apart, no matter the reason, we feel it's our fault."

Consciously, we may know it's not our fault, but Manfred is right that we biologically or subconsciously think we have failed, and shame around this often leads to depression. Unfortunately, society often perpetuates that sense for us. "I'm sorry your marriage failed," people say, or "It must be so hard to be alone." Even once I learned to say (and believed), "My marriage didn't fail; we succeeded in getting out before it became hostile," I still felt shame about how long it took me to process the divorce.

"Why am I still talking about this?" I complained to a friend while walking around Green Lake in Seattle. "My divorce was almost three years ago."

"If you got a new job three years ago, do you think you wouldn't talk about it? Or once your child is three, do you stop talking about her?" she laughed. "Divorce isn't an isolated event that only occurs for one day. You're going to be talking about it for years."

When I groaned, she said, "It's not as if that's all you'll talk about, it's just one aspect of your life."

She was right. I talked about my divorce for far longer than I'd anticipated, but that's not necessarily a negative thing. As long as I didn't feel shame about this or judge how long or severe each of the phases was, I could trust that my healing was occurring just as it should. And that eventually I would reach that golden meadow full of daisies called acceptance.

Acceptance

After years of getting knocked sideways by my emotions, I stopped being surprised by them. Instead of thinking, "Phew! That's over," as I used to after a round of anger or depression, I would think, "I wonder what the next round will be like?" I no longer thought in terms of "if," but rather "when." I reminded myself that acknowledging the problem and mood was leading me to acceptance, and that I had survived enough anger and grief phases to know I would survive the next one.

I didn't merely need to learn to accept my divorce, I also needed to learn how to accept people for who they are, not who I wanted them to be; to accept my life for what it was, rather than focusing on the next thing that would supposedly make it better; and most of all, to accept myself. Because if I didn't accept myself as I was, I couldn't accept others for who they were. And if I couldn't do that, I would continue to have unhealthy relationships and dissatisfaction.

Dawn Bradley Berry explains the acceptance phase as the final phase of healing "where the pace of life slows and people begin to achieve a sense of comfort and belonging in their new lives. The value of letting go of the past becomes clearer and the ability to trust begins to be restored. A new identity and a new focus, emerge."

I'd be lying if I said sadness or anger never resurfaced during the acceptance phase. They made appearances, but they were short-lived. Contentment was the overriding emotion. For those who love excitement, contentment can be excruciating, because the highs and lows are much smaller than they'd like. Honestly, boredom came hand-in-hand with contentment for me, but I learned to live with and accept it as well. For me, it was a far better place to be than on the roller-coaster ride of emotions. Because I learned that although it appeared that nothing (or very little) was occurring during contentment, that wasn't true. Contentment meant that I let go of my regrets about my past and fears about my future. It meant I was no longer driven by fear, sadness, or anger. It allowed me to know that my work, kids, life, relationships, and healing were exactly where they needed to be, even if that wasn't an ideal place. It meant I accepted myself and those who were in my life as being who they are, rather than who I hoped they (and I) would be. And this served me far better than any distraction or excitement ever did.

CHAPTER 7

THE OTHER DIVORCES IN YOUR LIFE

YOUR DIVORCE IS NOT AN ISOLATED INCIDENT; it may affect other areas of your life and many other people as well. Some people may shy away from you during this time because divorce makes them uncomfortable. And you may question some of your relationships as well because they'll remind you of your relationship with your ex. The patterns and problems you had with your ex were probably not limited to your marriage. If you're an enabler, you're probably also enabling family members, your boss, your kids, or friends. If your ex was a rageaholic, you probably have a family member or friend who also inappropriately and unjustly rants and rages around you. If your ex was any other kind of "aholic," (workaholic, alcoholic, etc.) you probably have other people in your life who don't properly address and deal with their emotions, but rather suppress them through work, television, porn, or substance abuse.

The good news: you don't have to hire a lawyer to divorce these people. The bad news: you still need to divorce them. But I hope you are learning through this book that all divorces are not created equal, and they can be done in a variety of ways. Similarly to how you are learning to create boundaries with your ex, you can do the same with other people. Knowing whether you need to divorce the person or the relationship is tricky, and I didn't always get it right the first time. But with practice, it became easier, as I hope will be true for you.

Take Note, but Don't Necessarily Act

As I've said, I wasn't always the most rational person while going through my divorce, and you may not be either. And that's all right. Be gentle with yourself, check in with yourself as often as possible, and remember: even our mistakes sometimes end up being gifts when we learn from them.

Before divorcing Jeremy, I divorced my agent, which was perhaps a mistake. After two years of working with her, we had a lot of praise and interest from an editor at Penguin Group, but no firm contract. I was frustrated by some of my agent's advice, which seemed to contradict the editor's advice, but overall I liked her and thought she worked hard to try to sell my novel.

I hired a mentor to help me with the manuscript, and on a bleak, grey, rainy day, she said, "Are you sure you want to keep working with this agent? Your job is to write the books, her job is to sell them. She didn't sell your memoir and now it seems as if she's losing interest in selling the novel. That's not doing her job. I'd fire her."

"But she works hard on submitting them," I countered. "We just haven't found the right editor."

"Again, that's her job and she's not doing it."

"It's probably just that the book sucks, that's why it's not selling."

"No, it's a good book."

I was frustrated by the publishing process, and perhaps somewhat with my agent, but more so at my marriage. The two became entangled and I let go of the safer person, the agent. Ultimately, I still had to let go of my husband, which left me with no husband and no agent.

With that word of caution, make sure you don't randomly start cutting people out of your life just as you're going to need support the most. I learned to pause (sometimes) before hitting the send key of an email that I may not be able to retract later. Rather than letting external advice overshadow my own instincts, I checked back in with myself. If you find yourself struggling with a boss, co-worker, friend, or family member, check in with yourself to see if it's really about that person, or if it's merely misplaced frustration about your divorce. If it's not about them, work out your issues by talking with someone else, journaling, or whatever outlets work best for you. If it is about them, try to do the impossible, which is to be rational. Fear, anger, and other emotions run high during divorce, so it is easy to over-react or feel overly sensitive.

During divorce, we learn that the problems in our marriage are rarely contained only in the marriage. If you can't stand to lose another person at this time, don't. You don't have to end all your unhealthy relationships while your marriage is ending. Merely take note of the pattern and address the issue when you are able.

Drift Away or Divorce?

I have frequently lamented the lack of a process or guide for unfriending friends. Before Facebook, we didn't even have a word for it. You didn't break up with a friend, nor did you divorce. Most likely, one of you merely stopped returning the other's calls and hoped she got the hint.

Most adults go through a series of evaluating their friendships as they age. In her 1992 study[7], Dr. Laura L. Carstensen's data shows that adults decrease their social interactions with acquaintances after the age of seventeen, increase them again between the ages of 30 to 40, then generally sharply decrease them from 40 to 50. She coined the term *socioemotional selectivity theory* to describe the tendency to spend more time on things and people we value and how our need to increase our social circle diminishes as we age.

Losing touch with friends or acquaintances because of a move or change of circumstance is often conflict-free because both parties have directed their attention elsewhere. Choosing to end a friendship is entirely different. And like the end of any relationship, it is often met with grief, awkwardness, or anger from the other party. A 2012 article in the *New York Times*, "It's Not Me, It's You" says, "Even though research shows that it is natural, and perhaps inevitable, for people to prune the weeds from their social groups as they move through adulthood, those who actually attempt to defriend in real life find out that it often plays like a divorce in miniature—a tangle of awkward exchanges, made-up excuses, hurt feelings and lingering ill will."

After my divorce, I started separating from a friend by claiming I was busy. This quickly felt wrong. I knew I owed her an explanation, so I told her how our relationship was a mirror of what was unhealthy in my marriage, and how I was discovering my codependent nature. Rather than focusing on myself, I was focusing energy on helping her. Yet this help often felt like judgment to her, because it was. I wasn't helping her—I was trying to fix her, which isn't healthy or possible. Even though we talked about this and tried to break the pattern several times, we were unsuccessful and slipped back to our old ways within a month. I started claiming I was busy again, but this time she saw through the excuses. "Are you divorcing me?" she asked. And my answer was yes.

In almost every example of defriending in the *New York Times* article, the defriender wrestled with guilt and/or sadness. Not returning phone calls made the defriender feel as if they had caused the ex-friend an unnecessary round of self-doubt. Yet the woman in the article who told her friend, "I wish you love, joy, peace and happiness but this friendship is over," also claimed to feel sad and guilty about divorcing her friend. Talking with my friend about our divorce rather than merely ignoring her seemed like the right thing to do, but I still felt sad.

I wish I could offer three simple steps to divorcing friends, but unfortunately, I believe it's not that easy. Every friendship is different. Sometimes, suggesting a break may be all you need. Maybe you really are busy right now or don't feel supported by this friend, but in a few months, you'll feel connected to her again. Ultimately, you know your level of comfort with honesty and you know your friend. Some people will move on and find other friends, but some won't. And maybe over time, you'll realize you didn't just want a break, you truly didn't want to be friends. For those people, even if it's difficult, I suggest a face-to-face conversation. The *New York Times* article advises a face-to-face talk, but if you can't do that, I suggest sending an honest letter or email. Keep the letter about yourself and your feelings rather than offering a list of accusations. If you give reasons why you cannot continue the friendship, make sure they are more about your feelings than placing all the blame on your friend.

As long as you explain your feelings and your need to take a break or not be friends, you can be reassured that you treated your friend and the situation with respect. Breaking up is never easy, and of course you'll feel sad or angry, but you don't need to feel guilty if you handled the situation with respect.

Maybe It's Not Over, Maybe It's Just Changing

Often rather than being best friends, you'd like to move your friend to an outer circle and become merely acquaintances. Or you may remain close, but don't see or talk to one another as often.

This is what happened with Jill and me. We were confidantes through our divorces and helped each other through an emotionally tumultuous time. We called each other our "surrogate husbands." When Jill entered a significant relationship, we stopped our weekly conversations. I was deeply hurt by what I perceived as "being dropped for a man." I almost let my mistaken sense of betrayal jeopardize our friendship and drafted several "if you don't have time for me, then you're not the friend I thought you were" letters in my head. Fortunately, I waited and actually called her when I was feeling more rational. I still confessed my hurt, but also admitted to being jealous because I felt I had been replaced.

Jill hadn't necessarily replaced me; her life had merely become too full. She worked more than fifty hours a week, her father was dying, she was selling her house, and she had entered a serious relationship. I still wanted a surrogate husband, but realized that wasn't healthy. I'd merely shifted my codependence from Jeremy to Jill. This awareness allowed me to shift from being hurt and angry about being "dropped" to seeing that she still cared and loved me, she just wasn't available for weekly or even monthly chats. Over the twenty years that I had known Jill, we had experienced times of frequent contact and other times where we didn't talk for a year. This didn't mean she wasn't a dear friend; it just meant our relationship ebbed and flowed over the years.

As my therapist explained, we have circles of people in our lives. The very center for me was my children, and that didn't change. But friends and lovers moved away from my core over time. This often felt lonely, and I complained about this feeling to my therapist.

"They're still in your life. They just aren't in the core," she reminded me.

"I want a full core," I said.

"Of course you do, but when your core was full of unhealthy relationships, you were still lonely. Now that you've created room in there you have the opportunity to fill it with new people who you have more in common with and are more emotionally on par with. And just because you make room for new people, doesn't mean you have to let go of everyone else. They're just not in your core anymore."

This made sense over time, and I no longer viewed time and space away from friends as losing them altogether. Usually, we merely took space from one another for a few months or changed the dynamic to being acquaintances rather than close friends. The benefit of divorcing friends as opposed to your husband: you don't have to drive to the bottom of the hill. You can drive halfway down or even park in the garage and think about it for a while. And when you're ready, you'll know what to do.

How Your Divorce May Affect Your Friends

My friend Sarah shared her feelings of betrayal and hurt when a friend stopped inviting her over after Sarah's divorce. "Mary's husband blames the divorce on me and is still friends with my ex, so Mary feels uncomfortable having me over because she doesn't want to run interference between her husband and me. She'll agree to coffee or a walk, as long as it doesn't involve going to her house or being around her husband."

Mary's "separate corners" philosophy was not only juvenile; it was meddling. Sarah and Mary's husband were not toddlers. They were adults who could work out their differences and be civil if allowed in the same room. I commiserated with Sarah and offered her my own experience. "Your divorce affects your friends as well. Give Mary some time. I think she'll come around once she becomes more comfortable with the situation."

Your divorce may trigger emotions in people in your world, and that may prevent them from being able to listen to you in the way you need. They might judge you, get angry, or even ridicule your decision or feelings. Obviously, you need to stop talking to these people about your divorce and seek out others. Again, that may involve paying a supportive, unbiased professional.

I was fortunate that none of my friends shunned me because of my divorce, but I certainly experienced distance with some friends. One was honest enough to say, "I don't know if I can get used to you being divorced. It freaks me out to hear about it." Her own parents went through a messy divorce when she was a teenager, so perhaps that contributed to her uneasiness later. Regardless, in my first year of divorce, it was too difficult for me to *not* talk about it, so I didn't see this friend very often. And when we did visit, we usually brought the kids as fodder for other topics to discuss. As time went on and I found other people I could talk freely with, it became more okay avoiding talking divorce with this friend. And as time went on, she also grew more comfortable with my divorce.

Another friend behaved similarly to Mary, but for different reasons. Her husband had never met Jeremy, so he certainly didn't side with him, but she no longer viewed me as a "family" or a "couple," so she stopped inviting me to "family" events. She invited me to dinner on my own, but I rarely was invited to her house. This confused me more than angered me, because I was still a mother. I still had a family. I also found it ironic, because most married couples I knew didn't talk to each other at parties anyway, so why would it matter if I wasn't accompanied by a spouse? With time, though, this friend and I were able to adjust our friendship so it satisfied both of our needs and comfort levels.

The Contagious Factor

Many women feel hurt—or at least confused—by the feeling of being dropped by friends after their divorce. "It's as if they think it's contagious," mused Susan, a forty-five-year-old divorcee with two adolescent boys. "How ridiculous is that?" I thought that was absurd as well until I read the 2011 *New York Times* article, "How Divorce Lost Its Groove" that suggested that the fear may not be unfounded. According to a study out of Harvard, Brown, and the University of California San Diego, "When close friends break up, the odds of a marital split among their friends increase by 75 percent."

I didn't notice a huge increase in my friends divorcing after I did, but almost all of my friends started analyzing their marriage. I was the first of my friends to divorce, and most of us had young kids at home. We were still preoccupied with finding time for sleeping, working, and, if we were really lucky, five minutes to ourselves. "I'm in survival mode," one friend admitted. "I don't have time to think about my marriage." A month or so after saying this, her marriage became the main topic of our dinner conversations.

Most of my friends' parents were divorced, and my friends remembered the bitterness all too well. As Susan Gregory Thomas explains in her book *In Spite of Everything*, most Gen Xers were shaped by their parents' divorce. She claims, "To allow our own marriages to end in divorce is to live out our worst childhood fears. More horrifying, it is to inflict the unthinkable on what we most love and want to protect: our children."

My divorce wasn't the same as my friends' parents' divorce. When I only periodically crumbled and then began to flourish, my friends saw their first role model of someone who got divorced without it ending their world. The unthinkable became thinkable, and most of them began to scrutinize their marriage. But awareness can be a selective process. In some cases, awareness caused positive changes, and the marriage improved. In others, it resulted in divorce. And in still others, it resulted in picking up the rock, looking at the creepy crawlies (the problems) underneath, and then putting the rock back down. "I can't afford to get divorced, so why bother even thinking about it?" one woman said.

"I was only making ten grand the year I got divorced, but I figured I couldn't afford to *not* get divorced," I replied. That woman didn't say much after that.

When Friends Divorce You

During their times of examining and not examining their own marriage, my friends' contact with me ebbed and flowed. I tried to not take this personally, viewing it as their own process. I knew all too well the ups and downs and bargaining phase of marriage. I also knew that often, people don't want to think about their marital problems, and being around me made them think about them. It wasn't an *A* emblazoned on my chest that they saw; it was a *D*. I trusted them and our friendship enough to know that wouldn't always be the case. Eventually, they would see Corbin again, not "divorce."

If they needed to pull away for a while, I accepted that. I tried not to analyze it or think it was due to something I had done, unless they told me otherwise. I didn't deem the friendship over, I merely viewed it as taking a break, or that maybe we were moving each other out a circle. Most of these moves were temporary. Most of my close friends, while still married, remain my close friends today.

A couple of friends divorced me by slipping away, but this might have happened over time anyway, even if I hadn't gotten divorced. Dawn Bradley Berry states in *The Divorce Recovery Sourcebook*, "In most cases, a few old relationships will fall by the wayside when a marriage ends. Be philosophical about this—there will be casualties with any major life change. Some friendships, just like some marriages, are wonderful for a time but are not destined to last forever."

How Your Divorce Affects Family Members

"Papa sees your parents as much as you do," my son observed one day. "And you never see his parents."

He was right about both situations. I attempted one or two visits with Jeremy's father and stepmother after our separation, but it was awkward for everyone, so we stopped initiating visits. Conversely, my parents continued to invite Jeremy to gatherings, talked to him regularly, and even included his picture in their Christmas newsletters. I didn't mind that they remained close to Jeremy, but I did mind that Jeremy still remained a part of our conversations, whereas the divorce and its effects were not. I didn't feel as if they took Jeremy's side or blamed me for the divorce, but I did feel as if they preferred to act as if it never happened. When they asked, "How's Jeremy?" I learned to reply quickly, "I don't know, ask him. We're divorced."

It was easier for them to not discuss the divorce. Or if it was discussed, they preferred to act as if it were for the best. Which it was, but that wasn't to say I didn't have complex feelings about it. My father routinely told his friends that Jeremy and I got along better now that we were divorced and that it wasn't that we ever had problems, we merely grew apart. "Actually Dad, that's not true," I said one night at dinner. "We did have problems, but it was hard for me to share them with people because everyone sees Jeremy as such a nice guy. And he is a nice guy, but it was really hard to live with him."

"Sure, kid, but it's not as if he cheated on you or lied to you."

"There are other ways to hurt people, Dad."

By claiming everything was fine and trying to keep things the same, no one—including Jeremy and me—was really adjusting to the divorce. On the day I filed my divorce papers, I cried to my mom, "I'm getting divorced." To which she said, "It's just a shift in your relationship, not an end." I felt saddened by her words, but didn't understand why. Then it hit me—she was negating and minimizing my feelings. True, Jeremy would still be in my life, but the bigger truth was I was getting divorced. I wanted and needed to mourn that.

Divorcing Family Members

As I said, the more you examine the patterns in your marriage, the more you will see some resemblance to your patterns with friends and family. Many theories of psychology, including the Imago Theory, claim that people seek partners who remind them of their primary caretakers and whom they can have a similar relationship with.[8] Your divorce can lead to some discomfort with your parents and extended family. Depending on the level of discomfort, you may need to take a break from your extended family, or you may want to divorce them entirely. Only you know what is right for you, and if you don't know yet, that's perfectly acceptable as well. You've let a very significant person go (your husband). You don't need to alter any other relationships right now if you're not ready.

During my divorce, I analyzed my relationship with my parents as well. This was rarely easy, but I viewed it as necessary. Jeremy did not resemble my father in many—if any—ways, but my relationship with my father had been strained for many reasons, including my perception of him as a bully. Emboldened by the courage it took to initiate a divorce, I began standing up for myself in all areas of my life, including with my father. Needless to say, this did not go over well. The ultimate conflict came the Christmas after my divorce when I told my father I would not be coming to their house. I had spent every prior Christmas traveling to my parents' house and this year, I didn't have the energy or inclination. With so much disruption and change occurring from the divorce, I wanted a calm, simple, intimate Christmas in my own home with my children. "Dad," I explained, "My whole life I heard you complain about going to your parents for Christmas."

"And that's why you have to come here," he yelled.

"No, I'm going to learn from your mistake, not follow it."

Angry emails ensued, followed by a standoff. My mother even told me my father was going to cut me out of his will, but I wouldn't relent. I was having Christmas at my house. After a month or so of silence from my father, he showed up at my house and said, "What's your beef with me, kid? Because trust me, I have some beefs with you."

"Really?" I asked. "You want to know?"

"Yes," he said. It was not our family pattern to openly discuss such things, but he had come to my house with this sole purpose, so I trusted that he was ready and open. We sat together in my living room for several hours and aired all of our "beefs." My father negated some of what I said and apologized for one thing. But primarily he listened, which is exactly what I wanted. I wasn't looking for apologies— I merely needed to express what I had felt silenced about my whole life.

I always think of my family when I read the children's book, *There is No Such Thing as a Dragon*. The mother in the book refuses to acknowledge the dragon living in her home, so the dragon becomes bigger and bigger, ultimately destroying the house. Finally, the little boy says, "There is a dragon" and pats it on his head. As soon as he does, the dragon shrinks down to kitten size. When the mother asks why it got so big, the boy responds, "I think it just wanted to be noticed."

By having my dad listen and acknowledge my grievances, the problems could shrink down to kitten size. We began talking more honestly with one another and respecting each other, rather than ignoring or negating one another. Rather than perceiving him as a bully, as I had previously, I started to appreciate and respect his direct manner of speaking. I even started to emulate it. And by standing up to him, I think he was able to respect me and see me for who I truly was, rather than the little girl I used to be, or who he wanted me to be. By standing up to him, I earned his respect, and I began respecting myself. From that point forward, I've been able to accept my dad for who he is and vice versa. Sure, we still tangle at times, but I view that as positive, because now we can listen to each other's viewpoints.

Melody Beattie, in *Language of Letting Go*, calls this "detaching with love." "Detachment means we care, about ourselves and others. It frees us to make the best possible decisions. It enables us to set the boundaries we need to set with people. It allows us to have our feelings, to stop reacting and initiate a positive course of action. It encourages others to do the same."

In order for two people to be able to overcome their conflicts, both parties need to be willing to acknowledge the other person's hurt and be willing to see their own part in it. This happened on that evening with my father and continued every time we had dinner together. Therefore, I didn't really divorce him; we merely abolished our previously dysfunctional relationship and replaced it with a healthier one.

Hopefully this can be the case with all of your divorces. But if it's not, and you need to divorce the person entirely, seek out support while doing so. Divorcing husbands, friends, and family members is stressful and sorrowful. Don't brave it alone.

Chapter 8

Valuing Your Alone Time

YOU MAY NOT BELIEVE THIS NOW, but according to Dominique Browning in her 2012 *New York Times* article, "Alone Again, Naturally":

> *Most single women I know really love their lives. We love doing whatever we want to do, when we want to do it. We love not being judged, not being criticized, not being hemmed in. We love the give and take of making our own decisions...*
>
> *A marriage is a lot of work. Strike that. A man is a lot of work. Anyone who has been in a bad marriage knows that its defining characteristic is the unspeakable loneliness in which one feels shrouded, a sense of isolation amplified by not being alone.*

Although I don't share Browning's (what I perceive as) negative thoughts about relationships, I do share her opinion on the joys of living alone. And according to a 2007 Census report, most divorced people took three and half years between their first and second marriages. For those 25 and older, 52 percent of previously divorced men and 44 percent of women were remarried.[9] And according to Dawn Bradley Berry in her *Divorce Recovery Sourcebook*, "Studies of middle-aged women, in particular, indicate that a majority report feeling better about themselves after a divorce was over. Few such women focus on finding a new husband. Many guard their hard-earned confidence and freedom fiercely."

Sociologist Eric Kleinberg states in his book, *Going Solo,* that people living alone make up 28% of Americans households—a larger percentage than any other domestic union including nuclear families. He claims these numbers are on the rise and are evidence of the biggest demographic shift since the baby boom. Even more surprising to some is that this demographic proves to be more engaged in social and civic life, debunking the myth that people living alone are isolated. Kleinberg's research shows that single people volunteer, take music and art lessons, and attend public events and lectures more often than their married counterparts and that there's even evidence that they are mentally healthier and live more sustainable lifestyles.

Alone and Lonely Are Not the Same

Many people equate alone time with being lonely. As Browning points out, many of us have already had our fill of being lonely even while married. We're convinced we'll be even lonelier while single and truly on our own. But alone does not have to mean lonely. It can mean that we are now free to enjoy our own company. We are given the chance and time to get to know and like ourselves again. Being alone can present many beneficial opportunities, but it's up to us how we perceive and spend our time by ourselves.

Florence Falk, in her book *On My Own: The Art of Being a Woman Alone,* explains that being alone is a neutral state; only our preconceived negative connotations make it seem bad. "Aloneness is part of the human condition. One of the ways to get in touch with ourselves is to really enter aloneness, from there finding our way to solitude. It is frightening at first. You need to reframe it to get over that fear. Think of the experience of peace you get walking on a beach, reading, taking yoga, anywhere there's silence and not a lot of distractions."

Listen to the Brain in Your Belly

When I first separated from Jeremy, I accepted several invitations from strangers or acquaintances because I was looking to expand my friendships. Within twenty minutes of being in someone's company I didn't particularly enjoy, my back hurt and my stomach tightened. While walking with an acquaintance one night, I thought I was getting the flu. Once I realized I was being talked at and lectured, I ended our time together. As soon as I left, the flu-like symptoms disappeared.

As I've said before, my brain was not always my ally; sometimes it lied to me. But my gut never lied. While my brain said, "It's good for me to explore new friendships," my gut screamed, "But not like this one! You're not being heard, let's get out of here."

Trusting your gut is not New-Age speak or hocus pocus. It's scientifically proven that 80 to 90 percent of the human body's total serotonin is found in specialized cells in our guts, not in our brains. In many species, including us humans, serotonin is key in the functioning of gut muscles, causing contraction of our intestines. As it turns out, our digestive system has its own neural network and largely controls itself without any input from our brains whatsoever.[10] Phillip Shepherd, author of *New Self, New World,* calls this the brain in our belly or pelvic brain. His research claims that philosophers have recognized this second brain from as early as 700 BC, and scientists have known about it since the early 1900s.

The negative encounter with the acquaintance was another reminder of what I already knew: being in bad company felt lonelier than being alone. By listening to the brain in my belly and ending the evening early, I was able to salvage the evening in a self-caring way. Spending time on your own can be nurturing as well as an excellent time to become familiar with your brain in your belly, and can even be a first step towards listening to and understanding yourself again.

Dating Yourself

Erica Manfred in her book *He's History, You're Not* describes women's need to be alone after a separation as "the freeze and hide stage." Rather than fight or flight, many newly divorced women freeze and hide in their homes as a way to recover. She reassures women that feeling as if they don't want to leave the house is certainly scary, but normal. "You are simply adjusting to a major traumatic change in your life, where pulling back is an essential part of the grieving process. You have the right to hide in your cave for as long as you need to and come out only when you're ready. In fact you may need to be alone to process what has happened to you. That processing, being honest with yourself, is the long-term remedy for loneliness."

While healing from my divorce, I realized my alone time felt different than it had in the past. As a child or while contemplating divorce, I often spent time alone as an escape or a way to avoid people or activities. Once I divorced, my alone time became a choice, rather than an escape. I actively scheduled time to engage with myself. And while "dating myself," I paid attention to myself and became in tune and learned to trust the brain in my belly. I didn't clean the house or try to accomplish tasks during these dates. I nurtured myself and treated myself to doing nothing, if that's what I wanted, or a pleasurable activity, if that's what I desired.

These dates with myself were what carried me through the work week. I viewed them as gas pumps where I filled myself not only for work, but more importantly, for my kids. I took care of myself and met my needs during this time, so I could be present when my kids returned home. If I didn't have my alone time on Sunday, I was burned out by Wednesday. And just like all dates, not every Sunday was orgasmic or even enjoyable. Sometimes I was awful company because I was lethargic and depressed. Sometimes I was cranky, and everyone— including myself—annoyed the hell out of me. But again, the beauty of *my* time was that I was able to be in whatever mood I was in. I didn't have to stuff it for my kids' or anyone else's benefit. I could cry, laugh hysterically, swear, or just lie around for as long as I needed to.

One thing that makes being alone so scary is that you are forced to be alone with your feelings. Sure, you can watch movies, play music, and be as busy as you want, but eventually it's just you and your thoughts. And that is what is so terrifying. Especially after something as difficult as a divorce, most people don't want to think. They want to be distracted. But distractions won't heal you so you can move on. Only being honest with yourself will.

Ask Yourself Questions

Part of being honest means getting to know yourself again as *you*, not as a mother and wife. Who are you? What are your likes and dislikes? What parts of yourself have you given up since marriage? What parts would you like to reclaim? Reacquainting yourself with you takes time. You didn't lose yourself instantly, so you won't find yourself instantly, or even in a few weekends. Plus, the new you is probably unknown at this point. Sure, you may have relived your twenties for a bit after your divorce—I certainly did—but I knew this wasn't the real me. I had to go back to that time in my life and relive it because it was the last time I was solely Corbin. I wasn't a wife or a mother, I was just me—free to be, think, and do almost whatever I wanted. After reacquainting myself with her, I kept the parts I liked about twenty-something Corbin and left the rest behind. I kept the ability to be spontaneous, along with the view that the world was full of possibilities, not limitations.

Once I had a sense of who I was, it was time to look at how and why I lost that Corbin. For many women, this is where blame and rage come in. We blame our ex for changing us or limiting us. Or we cling to who we were as a wife, still want to be a wife, and again blame our ex for ruining or walking out of our marriage. As I explained in chapter six, all feelings are valid, but rage also prevents us from looking at our part in how things happened. Even if your ex lied and cheated, you had your part in the relationship. Hence, the term "relationship," meaning "behavior or feelings towards someone else." He wasn't single while your relationship dissolved; you were married to him. Whether you looked the other way, nagged him incessantly about his faults, or became a martyr, you played a part in your marriage's dynamics.

Owning Your Part of the Divorce so You Can Move On

This is where you need to sit down and have an honest talk with yourself. What was your role in the marriage? What parts of that role did you like? What didn't you like? How can you avoid being the martyr, victim, over-compensator, screaming lunatic, or any other negative role again? Were you always hoping he would be someone he wasn't? Did you marry his potential, not who he actually was?

Did you know of his faults, but think he would be different with you? Were you trying to control him? How did you become that way? How can you get your needs met and set healthy boundaries so you don't have to resort to those ineffective tactics again? These and many more self-reflective questions may feel uncomfortable, but they are mandatory. To heal, you can't blame him for all of the problems in the marriage. You need to see your part as well.

We cling to rage and blame at times because it keeps us company, but who wants that kind of companion? Erica Manfred says, "As long as we can feel it (anger), we're not faced with the terror and emptiness of being alone. To me that anger is a warmth in the gut, a way of feeling alive instead of cast adrift. However, you never get to enjoy your life if you're too busy being angry at someone who doesn't matter to you anymore."

I wouldn't suggest spending the weekend alone with your resentment and anger. You want to start to view yourself as a loving, lovable being, which is rarely possible while isolating yourself with your anger. Kick resentment and anger to the curb and invite honesty and self-reflection in instead. Once you become comfortable seeing yourself as you truly are and owning your part in the divorce, it's time to forgive yourself. Yes, you made mistakes, but whoever said you were supposed to be perfect? No one did. (Okay, maybe you did, but you were wrong.) The beautiful thing about awareness is that it is the first step towards healing. The horrible thing about awareness is that you no longer have rage and denial as your bedmates. But they were horrible lovers anyway, remember?

Being aware of your part in your marital strife is the first step towards breaking the pattern for future relationships. Even if dating is not on your agenda (and I recommend it not be until at least six months, if not a year, after you separate), at some point in time you will want some sort of companionship. And even if you never date again, you are still in relationships with people. The patterns you had with your ex will start playing out with your relationship with your kids, a friend, or colleague. In order to prevent that, it's important to date yourself, get to know yourself again, forgive yourself, love yourself, and begin to heal from your divorce.

What Do I Do On My Weekends Alone?

My favorite way to spend a Saturday evening was with a close friend, sitting on one of our couches eating, chatting, and maybe having a glass of wine. I spent a lot of time doing this. I also encouraged myself to go to parties where I wouldn't know anyone, or to go hear music. Sometimes I didn't have energy to be social, but at the same time, I didn't want to be alone. On these nights, the women-only Korean spa was the perfect solution. I was comforted by the female chatter all around me while still enjoying the meditative, restorative time I needed.

Once I became comfortable being anonymously alone at the spa, I added going out to eat by myself as an acceptable way to spend a Saturday. In the past, I had viewed dining alone as sad and awkward, but then I mastered the art of eavesdropping. I loved listening to the stilted date taking place next to me and thinking, "Phew! Glad that's not me." I'd jot down column ideas, steal interesting dialogue for a future story, or just pretend to be writing while really listening to every word the diners said next to me.

Jill offered another view on how to spend the potentially lonely night *not* being lonely. "You know what I did last Saturday?" she said over the phone. "I bought a nice bottle of wine, blasted some eighties music, danced and sang around the house, and basked in the fact that no one was around to make fun of me. It was awesome!"

"I love it!" I squealed. "I have to remember this is a gift; I'm totally free to do whatever I want. I won't be alone forever, so I should relish these nights. And treat myself to them."

I can't say I never spent another Saturday night feeling anxious or sad, but those nights were rare. Usually, I asked myself what I wanted for the weekend. If it was quiet decadence, I bought some rich cheese, savory salmon, and exotic greens to make myself a special dinner. I ran a steamy hot bath, complete with lavender-scented bubbles, and relished being able to stay in there (uninterrupted and without toys being offered to me) for as long as I wanted. Sometimes I rented a movie for myself, sometimes I got out my watercolors, and sometimes I knitted or wrote in my journal. And I always read a lot. I'm a voracious reader, but I felt apprehensive reading around my kids because they viewed a horizontal mom with a book in her hand as an invitation to pile on her and ask a thousand questions about the book.

The key was that I could do these activities without interruptions and without sharing. Both of those notions were novelties—I was a mother of two young children, after all. Paint with my special watercolors bought only for me, not messy eager children? What a luxury! Eat a pound cake all by myself and not have to share? And be able to do so while leisurely lying on the couch, not hiding in a bathroom and stuffing it in my mouth as quickly as I could so my kids wouldn't see it? Orgasmic! These simple—but decadent—pleasures kept me happy and content for quite a while.

Reacquaint Yourself with Your Hobbies and Interests

Besides eating entire pound cakes peacefully, I asked myself what were some of the hobbies or pleasures that I had given up since marriage and motherhood. Taking classes was something I'd continually said I wanted to do, but I'd never found time. Well now, I had the time. I enrolled in a salsa class for several months. Although I enjoyed the class and especially the music tremendously, I suck at salsa. The teacher humored me, while continually scolding me in her beautiful rolling "rrrs" way, "Stop leading! You are not the man."

"I have control issues," I commented back.

"I can tell," she said as she spun me in a very complicated twist made more difficult because my arm was not fluid; it was ramrod straight. Although my hips never swiveled like hers and my body didn't sway and flow, I had a great time. An added bonus: lots of men took the class, so I could practice talking to and even touching (yikes!) the opposite sex.

I moved on to yoga, something I suck less at, and then belly dancing. (You guessed it—I totally sucked at that.) Sometimes I took drawing classes or a mosaic class. I chose the classes purely for their joy factor. I didn't care if I become good at any of these things. I just wanted to experiment and have fun.

Hiking was another thing I reclaimed after my divorce. Hiking with my kids was not hiking. It was walking and stopping to look at rocks and leaves every five seconds. Jeremy was not a big hiker either, and finding five free hours when the kids were young was about as easy as discovering the cure for cancer. But now I had the time and luxury to spend a day finding a trail and huffing and puffing my way up it. Even if I swore along the way, which I often did, I could do so without offending little innocent ears. I knew myself well enough to know that the best part of hiking was eating a ton and taking a bath afterwards. "But you ate and took baths every Saturday!" you say. True, but I found it especially rewarding after exerting myself. My sore muscles made me feel proud and especially worthy of the Fettuccine Alfredo I gobbled down afterwards.

When I slipped into a "What do I do with myself now?" state or felt self-pity, I reminded myself that all I had to do was make it through Saturday night. Sundays were always easier. I love to sleep in—another impossibility with kids. The mere thought of being able to wake when I wanted to, not when someone wanted pancakes, made my spine tingle. I was crazy about sleeping and quite good at it as well. With that carrot dangling, sometimes I merely got through Saturday any way I could.

Sundays were my spiritual days. I spent them relaxing and puttering. "Shoulds" were banned from Sundays, making it a very uplifting, rather than punitive spiritual practice. Besides resting and nurturing myself, two outside influences played a large role in making Sundays spiritual: my yoga class and my 12-step meeting. Both of these places allowed me to have the safe, cozy, true-to-myself alone feeling while being in the company of others. I could talk or not talk, but I always learned something from both groups.

Experiment with the New You: What Does She Want?

Cheryl Strayed's description of "alone" in her memoir, *Wild,* perfectly describes my feeling. "Alone had always felt like an actual place to me, as if it weren't a state of being, but rather a room where I could retreat to be who I really was." All day and weeklong I focused on my kids, my clients, my writing, traffic, the grocery store, and so on. And in doing so, Corbin would become lost again. Not as lost as when I was married, but still under a few layers of dirt. Saturday was when I brushed those layers off and turned my attention inward. It offered the time and place where I reconnected with myself and asked: are you being true to yourself? Are you working towards your goals at a reasonable pace? Are you letting other's needs come before yours? What do you want right now? What do you want a year from now? How can you make that happen for yourself? What areas of your life are you grateful for? Which areas still bother you? Should you do something about it or just trust that it will take care of itself?

These and many more thoughts circulated around my head and helped me grow my career, become financially stable, work on my emotional issues, and form a support network and deepen friendships. But even more important, I learned to understand myself and focus on my needs rather than merely focusing on others. The biggest goal I had for myself after divorcing was to never, ever let my inner compass go awry and untended again. I often thought of the image on the cover of James Frey's *Million Little Pieces*. Rather than all of the little pieces of my life breaking apart, I felt as if they were now coming towards me to make a whole. During my alone time, I made myself whole again.

For my friend Faith, dating herself led her to decide to go back to school. Several years after her divorce, she enrolled in nursing school. She laughed that it would give her something to do while her daughter was at her father's, but I knew it was much more than that. Faith was looking for stability, something she hadn't had in her marriage or her career as a freelance writer. She wanted to support herself and her daughter without help. Her ex was spotty with his child support, so Faith didn't want to depend on it. She spent a lot of time with a therapist—and alone—to get to know herself again and learn how she could regain the confidence that was shattered during her divorce. Financial stability would be a huge step towards feeling safe and confident again.

I didn't see Faith for over a year while she was in school. Yes, she was studying hard for her nursing degree, but she was also continuing to study herself without being distracted by friends or dating. She wasn't choosing to be alone forever; she was merely taking a couple of years to improve her life—and therefore her daughter's life—by focusing on herself and her financial stability. And by doing so, if and when she dated, she could be more confident that she wouldn't choose another unhealthy partner, because she was no longer the same person. And she wouldn't lose herself in him, because she had worked hard to create a fulfilling life and career for herself.

Manifestos

In *The Good Karma Divorce*, Judge Michele Lowrance describes how she has all litigants filing for divorce in her courtroom write their Personal Manifesto. The Manifesto allows people to express their fears, hurts, and anger on the page, while also requiring they state their goals for the divorce and for after the divorce. Since divorce initiates a multitude of changes and opportunities, she believes referring to the Personal Manifesto will help people choose growth over stagnation or compassion over bitterness. She quotes Nietzsche when describing this process: "The most spiritual men, as the strongest, find their happiness where others would find their destruction: their joy is self-conquest."

If your future is unclear to you at this point, that's all right. You can still create a Manifesto. Rather than having concrete goals—such as "Find a new job that pays me $70,000 a year"—you may have "a sense of security" as your goal. There is no such thing as a wrong goal, and the goals can shift over time. As Lowrance says, "Whether your mission is your personal enlightenment, protecting your soul from permanent wounds, or minimizing the damage to your children, you will be able to make sense of the tumultuous present and develop a view of the past that gives the future meaning... Your Manifesto will become a sanctuary, a refuge, where you will be protected from the onslaughts of polluted thoughts about your divorce."

Take some time to create a Personal Manifesto and keep it. As Lowrance says, your Manifesto can have personal goals on it as well as career or financial goals. Even if you don't accomplish all your goals, you will most likely accomplish some things of value. And rereading your Manifesto will be a great reminder of how much you have changed and grown as a person.

CHAPTER 9

GETTING THE SUPPORT YOU DESERVE

Divorce Buddies

IF YOU FEEL AS IF YOU CAN'T SPEND another weekend pondering your life, don't worry, you don't have to. Now that you've created space for new relationships, you will have them. You will have more time and energy because you will no longer be depleted by unhealthy relationships. You will also have clearer insights into what you really want and stronger boundaries on what you won't accept. As one woman recently told me, "When I feel pain now, I say 'ouch!' rather than thinking it's normal. When people don't respect me, I don't socialize with them. It sounds so basic, yet this shift has changed my life radically."

As I mentioned, I was the first of my friends to get divorced. Although my married friends were a huge support, I was desperate to talk to someone who had gone through the process of divorce. I wasn't very selective about whom I talked to. My only criteria were that they had experienced and survived a divorce. One day, my son's kindergarten teacher rested her hand on my arm sympathetically and said, "I heard you're getting divorced. I'm sorry, I just went through that."

"Really?" I asked. "Can we hang out sometime?" She agreed before I could judge myself for being inappropriate. We met for coffee a few days later when she honored me by sharing her story. Although her situation was more acrimonious than mine, I still learned a lot by talking with her. Her son was close to my son's age, and she offered a lot of suggestions on how to ease the transition from house to house each week. She didn't gloss over the bad parts, but she also wasn't withering from her divorce. She looked radiant and seemed happy. I learned later she was dating a man ten years younger, and I suspected that was contributing to her luminous glow.

A woman working at Trader Joe's asked me how I was one day. I blurted out, "I'm a mess. I'm getting divorced."

"I'm sorry. I got divorced last year; it was horrible."

"Really? But you seem all right now," I said.

"Sure, it's a year later," she laughed. She said she was about to take a break and asked if I wanted to walk with her to the coffee shop.

"Of course!"

That mere ten-minute exchange with her carried me through the week. I could tell by her smile and tone of voice that she meant it when she said, "It seemed like the end of the world when it happened, but now I'm actually grateful." I loved that she took time out of her day to reach out to a total stranger. People in Seattle are distantly polite. The joke amongst non-natives is that Seattleites say, "Let's get coffee," for five years before they actually set a date with you. But this woman, a total stranger, not only invited me to coffee, but she shared her story, vulnerabilities, inspiration, and fears with me. What a gift.

Eventually, I wanted more than an hour with a person. I wanted divorced friends I could talk to regularly. Many single women ask, "Where are all of the good men?" Similarly, I caught myself saying, "Where are all of the interesting divorced women?" And the answer was the same: "Busy with their rich lives." If I wanted to meet fascinating, intellectually stimulating, emotionally healthy people, I needed to go to fascinating, intellectually stimulating events such as readings, plays, or classes.

My first divorce buddy found me at one of my readings. Marcia approached me wearing a jester's hat, cat-eye glasses, and a mischievous grin. Her own divorce was finalized that day and she was out celebrating. "I think I may be getting divorced too," I told her, which was the first time I had ever spoken those words out loud or even internally to myself.

"I know you are," she said. "I also know we're going to be friends. I'll be your divorce buddy."

I found Marcia's candidness refreshing. Being at a literary event, where people tend to be reserved and serious, made me appreciate this jovial, prophet woman with bells on her head all the more. We became instant friends, and just like she predicted, she helped guide me through my divorce. Marcia offered advice and insight, but even more importantly, she was proof that I would make it through the ordeal. She was also an artist, so when not processing my divorce, I enjoyed brainstorming creative ideas with her and talking about our dreams and plans for our work. An unexpected bonus was she was a gateway to other single women.

Marcia invited me to a party on the same day Jeremy rented a U-Haul to move the rest of his belongings from my house. I told her no way. The kids and I were grieving. In actuality, the kids were dancing and spinning around our almost furniture-less living room saying, "Look at all of the room we have now! We should give all of our furniture to Papa!"

"Doesn't sound as if they're grieving to me," Marcia said. "Call a babysitter and I'll be there in an hour to pick you up."

I stared incredulously at the phone. Where was my sympathetic friend who smoothed my hair when I was crying and fetched me a blanket, or even better, made me fresh guacamole? I couldn't go to a party with her; I was mourning the loss of my marriage. And so were my kids. I needed to be there with them. Just then, my son showed me a Wiffle ball covered in cat hair. You would think it was a treasure chest by the way he beamed. "It must have been stuck under the couch. I've been missing this!" he said.

I had to admit to myself then that the kids were not currently grieving and that maybe they didn't need me to stay home. In fact, maybe I had been hyper-focused on them and their "process," and the best thing for all of us was for me to get out of the house for a few hours. I asked them if they were all right with their favorite babysitter, Jenn, watching them that night. They responded by holding a dance party in her honor.

"Family" Can Mean Many Things

When Marcia pulled up an hour later, I ran out to meet her with a bottle of wine in my hand and a smile on my face.

"I don't know where we're going or anyone at the party, do I?" I asked her.

"No, dearie, you don't, and that's a good thing," she responded.

It was the first party I'd been to in fifteen years as a single woman. I was completely unnerved to be there without Jeremy, my kids, or even a wedding ring, but within five minutes I met three other single women. One was getting divorced, one never married the father of her child (though he sporadically kept in touch with her and their son), and one was divorced and now in a new relationship with a man with a daughter. Almost everyone I met that evening was in some sort of unconventional relationship, and everyone was learning how to make it work for themselves and their "family."

That party solidified what I thought, but up until then hadn't found proof of: another life was possible for me. A life that perhaps didn't include a nuclear family, but a life in which I could grow and flourish while still being a mom. At the party Marcia took me to, and many similar parties I attended afterwards, I learned a variety of ways people made their new lives work for them. I met other single moms, women who lived with their boyfriends, girlfriends, roommates, or even alone. The idea of "family" expanded beyond man, wife, and children to include relatives, friends, or merely one parent and a child. And through these men and women, I felt validated as a family again.

Genevieve Clapp, in her book *Divorce and New Beginnings*, recommends reaching out to other single people as soon as possible, because "for many singles, the friendships formed after divorce are the closest and most rewarding they have ever had. Some have friends who are basically surrogate families..." My divorced friends became my surrogate family: the people I reached out to, spent Thanksgiving with, and most of all, the people who showed me I was still a family and I could make this new life work for myself and my kids.

Let Things Go

My friend Wendy, in particular, regularly reminded me of the importance of letting go when feeling overwhelmed.

"I can't do this—it's too hard," I'd complain to her.

"You *are* doing it," she reassured me. "What can you let go of for today?"

I was working more and I didn't share a home with a partner, so there was no way I could keep up with my pre-divorce standards. In my married life, while Jeremy or I made dinner, the other one would play with the kids. If one child had to be at school early for a field trip, Jeremy would drop the child off while I got the other one ready. I resisted and resented not being able to be there for both of my kids, but in reality, I was now outnumbered. And when I tried to do everything myself, I became overwhelmed at best, frustrated and angry at my worst. I was going to have to let some of my standards slide.

One day I complained to Zoe about my son being home sick—but not sick enough to stop asking me every five minutes what I was doing. "That's what videos are for," Zoe calmly responded. I began my anti-television diatribe, but she cut me off. "So they watch a video every once in a while. It's not going to rot their brains immediately. You don't even have cable and all you have are PBS videos! How damaging can *Clifford the Dog* be?"

My son was almost seven at the time and had never seen commercials or a Disney movie, not to mention anything remotely violent. Not at my house, anyway—his father had different rules and standards. I laughed at how absurd I was being and put a National Geographic movie in the DVD player.

Jill continually bragged about cereal night. She viewed it as a true sign that she had been liberated from many of her "shoulds." "Cereal night rocks!" she boasted. "Total prep and clean up time is about 5 minutes and the kids love it." I followed her lead and simplified all of my meals to include not more than twenty minutes of prep time. When even that felt too arduous, we ordered Thai food.

Let Your Friends Help

Letting things go became easier, but I still wasn't comfortable asking for practical help from others. Emotional help was different somehow. I readily called friends to talk, but I rarely, if ever, asked them to physically help me. I assumed everyone was strapped for time and resources, so I didn't want to burden my friends. Although my life felt like a house of cards, I still thought that precarious house was up to me to handle. Solina Ricci in *Mom's House, Dad's House* calls this being in a closed system, rather than in the preferable extended or open-style family. In closed systems, the adults reach out only to their spouse and maybe one other adult for help. They feel responsible for all of the family's needs. "The difficulty with this closed system is that families have many personal needs, many responsibilities, and too little time for fun and for enjoying one another. For some families, it becomes a merciless cycle where there are too many needs and too few people to meet them."

I was in a closed system. After weeks of swearing at traffic and running late to pick up the kids, I finally admitted to myself, "I can't keep doing this. It isn't working for any of us." I arranged a carpool with a neighbor and learned that it was all right to call another mom when I was running late to ask her to greet my kids at school. I learned that it was all right to invite ourselves over to a friend's house when I was feeling stressed, in need of adult company, or as if cooking and cleaning up after a meal was about as desirable as shoving hot spikes into my eyes. I released myself from being the center and sole person responsible for all of my family's needs. In short, I became comfortable asking friends for emotional and physical help.

What was arduous for me is perhaps not arduous for others, and vice versa. I was almost always willing to have a houseful of kids, but I rarely viewed that as "helping." It wasn't until a friend said, "You always have a host of kids with you. How do you do it?" that I realized this was an area where I could reciprocate and help my friends. After surveying several of them, I discovered that some viewed hosting play dates as a chore, and they would much rather make dinner for me. "Deal!" I squealed. "I hate cooking." Learning about my friends' gifts, talents, and willingness, as well as my own, allowed me to open my closed system to one that resembled an extended family.

Friends as Role Models

Ricci explains that extended families are good for parents and kids because they offer multiple role models for the divorced family, which may feel as if it became very small, very quickly. I regularly got together with the single moms I met through Marcia, not only for us, but so our kids could be around other divorced families as well. I loved the influence these other women had on my children, who had been relatively isolated, having come from a closed family. Marcia quickly became my daughter's "special friend" and she often gifted my daughter with shiny objects and designed art projects for her. Ricci describes these adult friends as someone to show new skills and tricks to, sit quietly with, or "gradually become a mentor, or an adopted uncle or aunt."

For me, these other adults and their children also offered a sense of normalcy for my family. None of us were part of a nuclear family anymore, but all of us were still a family. During one of the first dinners we had together, a little four-year-old boy announced, "I have two homes."

"So do all of the kids here," I responded.

"Yay for two homes!" Marcia cheered.

All of the other kids cheered with her until the four-year-old said, "I don't like it. It makes me sad."

"Yes, that's true too," Marcia said. "But you know what? Everyone in this room knows about the difficulties of two homes and missing a parent, so if you ever want to talk about it, we're here."

He smiled and resumed throwing balls at the other kids.

I don't recall the kids ever sitting in a corner counseling one another, but I know fragments of their new lives came out while they played. They expressed anger at having to be at one parent's house over a holiday they would have rather spent with the other parent. Or they'd say it was confusing as to where they were supposed to be every week. Even if the kids didn't discuss their parents' divorce, it was incredibly valuable to be among kids who had experienced something similar, so they didn't feel alone.

Kids Helping

These women also showed me how my kids could take on more responsibilities. While on a camping trip with Marcia, I watched in awe as her seven-year-old son set up the tent on his own and agreed to go on a six-mile hike. My kids thought tent poles were giant toy swords and complained when we walked five blocks to the park. I opted to go on the hike by myself that trip, but my kids did learn how to put a tent up. Other divorced friends' elementary school-aged kids did their own laundry, helped make dinner (and by helped, I mean actually *cooked*, not just got in the way), and walked the dog. This was not the norm in my middle-class Seattle neighborhood where there was usually a stay-at-home mom. I knew five-year-olds who still needed help going to the bathroom and getting dressed, and some neighborhood kids balked when I asked them to clear their plates. I wanted my kids to be confident and independent, and I certainly didn't want to be a martyr mom. In order to prevent this, we started sharing more of the household responsibilities.

The kids acclimated quickly, because they were young enough to think helping in the kitchen or making their own lunches was fun. When it started to feel more like a chore—which it was—they protested. Fortunately, by then I was mostly over my guilt about not being Super Mom and had learned to accept that I couldn't do it all: the kids simply had to help. By watching some of my single friends interact with their kids in a manner that was more of a partnership, I started to preach the same doctrine.

"We're a family and that means we all help out in ways that we can. I don't necessarily feel like making dinner, but I do, because that's my responsibility. Your responsibility is to put your laundry away, clear off all of your school stuff from the table, and set the table. Chores aren't always fun, but they still need to get done."

Their school was too small to have the option to buy lunch, so I passed lunch-making to the kids. We made it as entertaining and fair as possible: they made their lunch while I cleaned up from dinner, and we could catch up while working together. Responsibilities such as picking up after themselves and doing their own dishes were standard everyday occurrences, but along with them came a chore chart with a rotating weekly responsibility. Feeding the cat, sweeping the kitchen, vacuuming, watering the plants, and unloading the dishwasher were options, and each kid chose which chore they wanted for the week. This enabled a sense of choice and control for the kids and removed me from the dictator/martyr role.

Paid Support

Friends are invaluable, especially when you're in transition. But at times, you may need more support than they can offer. I've cleaned friends' houses for them when they were sick, but I wouldn't do it every month. I'll watch their children for them after school, but I don't want to be their full-time nanny. Identify the areas in your life you feel most taxed by and explore ways to release yourself from some of those burdens.

I needed help with childcare and cooking. For two years, we had a roommate who watched the kids for me at times in exchange for discounted rent. She became a member of our household and we loved her. I also received the extra income I needed and didn't have to incur childcare expenses. She moved out eventually, and although we were devastated, we found a different tenant/babysitter who loved to cook! He also had reliable transportation, something our other roommate lacked.

For years I yearned to be the dad in the family. I wanted to walk out the door in the morning, go to work uninterrupted, and return home to a happy family and a meal on the table. This probably occurred three times while I was married. But now, every Wednesday I was able to work a full day without worrying about picking up the kids, grocery shopping, or cooking. It was heaven!

When household maintenance became too much for me, I called my contractors. They lived up the street from me, were incredibly sweet, offered me ridiculously low rates, and even made coffee in the morning. Although gardening is something I enjoy, and it relaxes me, the first year after my divorce I felt overwhelmed by tending a garden. So I hired someone to help me. Yes, he too was reliable, inexpensive, and sweet. And even better, he always had a smile on his face and he whistled while he worked. His presence lifted my spirits. Watching him remove garbage cans full of weeds and dead plants allowed my shoulders to relax for the first time in months.

At times, your friends may help you with these tasks. My friend Cindy is the master of organizing work parties at her house. But for me, I already felt as if I relied on my friends for so much emotional support, I didn't want to task them further by asking them for household support. Plus, there's something clean and efficient about paying someone. At a time in my life when very little felt clean or efficient, I valued the structure and straightforward understanding of my hired relationships over the messiness of asking for favors and doing trades.

Therapists

Another area in which you might want to consider seeking professional help is with a therapist. As Dawn Bradley Berry advises, "Many psychologists who work with patients recovering from a divorce caution that the support of friends and relatives, while valuable, may not be enough, because such people lack the objectivity that a detached professional can offer." She explains that divorce brings out many unresolved issues from the past, so these areas may be best explored with a trained therapist. "The problems that arise in the fallout that follows a divorce are often deeper than the divorce itself," Bradley Berry says. "This may be a prime opportunity to learn more about yourself, work through old emotional issues, and gain insights that can make all the facets of your life happier and more fulfilling and enable you to build stronger relationships in the future."

In my liberal circle in Seattle, almost everyone saw or had seen a therapist. We spoke of them by first name, and several of my friends saw my therapist. When I sought counseling for my son he said, "Oh, like what you and Papa do." He wasn't ashamed or scared. He was even a bit excited. When I'd tell a mom he couldn't have a play date because he had an appointment, he'd tell his friend, "I'm going to see my counselor." He saw no reason for discretion.

If you want discretion, keep your therapist to yourself. No one needs to know you are seeing one, but please, don't feel as if seeing one means that you are broken. Being broken is keeping your problems to yourself; seeking therapy is a sign of strength. It also means you are on the path to healing yourself. Bradley Berry says, "There is no shame, no demonstration of weakness in seeking therapy or counseling. On the contrary, it takes wisdom to recognize and admit that you could benefit from assistance and strength to seek out the help you need."

When looking for a therapist, be discerning. Therapists rarely make you feel worse, but don't settle for feeling the same, either. The goal is to start feeling better, to accept yourself more, and to have faith in yourself and your future. My first therapist fell into the "fine" category. I learned some things from her, but quickly yearned to go deeper into my issues, which she shied away from. She moved out of town, allowing our relationship to end right at the time I was considering finding a different therapist.

My next—and last—therapist impressed me at our first meeting. She said, "I bet you talked circles around your other therapist. You could fill this room with words and are obviously an insightful woman, but you won't bowl me over." That was exactly what I wanted— someone to call me on my crap. Several friends claimed they would never see my therapist because they didn't want to be told what to do. They just wanted to be listened to. I understood that, but in my opinion, that's what my friends were for. I didn't spend money on a therapist to be politely heard; I spent it to receive advice and answers to my questions. I sought the kind of guidance friends can't provide, because they don't have the training or the background to understand the complexity of the issue. I went deep with my therapist in every session. If I didn't cry or leave with at least two "a-has," I felt as if it was a wasted session.

This intensity may not be what you want, and that's fine. But know what you do want before agreeing to work with someone. Interview several therapists, check their references and specialties, but then follow your intuition. Just like when meeting a new boss, colleague or friend, your gut usually tells you if it's going to be a good match or not.

If finances prohibit you from seeking counseling, see if your state offers assistance in that area. I qualify for subsidized health care for my children through Washington State's medical plan. Their insurance covered counseling, so I didn't have to pay for my son's therapy. My first therapist had a sliding fee scale, so I was able to receive counseling for a very reasonable rate.

Group Therapy

Another option for free or inexpensive emotional support is group therapy. I found several groups for divorced women, but settled on a 12-step program. I loved that group and relied on it every Sunday to help ground me. A room full of people from completely different backgrounds who experienced and expressed similar feelings and struggles was invaluable to me. "There's magic in the room," members often said, and it was true. It helped me feel less alone to hear the members share their stories. The first time I brought a friend with me, he said, "The depth and vulnerability expressed in that room is impressive, even intimidating, and I've been in a ton of groups like this."

Spiritual Support

A spiritual group or practice can help you during this time of transition as well. While there, ask if they have additional support for families in transition. The Internet also contains vast information about spiritual groups who offer emotional support and resources in your area. As Dawn Bradley Berry says, "Religious faith or other forms of spiritual foundation can be among the most important sources of comfort and stability for a person facing major life changes." She claims spiritual support can help put things in perspective, help with forgiveness and self-acceptance, and offer faith in a more positive future.

Before you think I'm pushing the Bible, church, or God on you, let me reiterate: I am a spiritual person, not a religious person. I won't dissuade you from seeking solace in church—if you find comfort there, great! But if you are wary of churches, try to be open to other spiritual places or practices. I consider my walks, 12-step group, yoga, and time in nature, all parts of my spiritual practice.

I included the kids in spiritual activities at times in order to provide them with a spiritual base in our non-religious home. We attended an earth-based spiritual temple where we made friends and were once again supported as a "non-traditional" family. We also conducted our own spiritual practices at home to help acclimate us during trying times or to celebrate. We often conducted rituals around letting things go or adding things to our life by writing these items on a piece of paper and either burning them (letting them go) or keeping them. Sure, my daughter often misunderstood this as a time to ask for a dog. I reminded her it wasn't necessarily a time to wish for an item, but rather to seek a feeling or a goal. The following month, "dog" would still make its way into our wishing bowl, but along with it would be "to make a friend at dance class."

Help From a Deity (or at least stop thinking you're God)

Although I believed in something besides humans controlling the earth and their destiny, I didn't know what these forces looked like or what they were. Sometimes, I pictured little fairies creating serendipities for me, sometimes I imagined a God or Goddess, but mostly they were ethereal. I believed in the idea of something, but never prayed to that thing nor thought to ask it for help. I bristled when I heard people in my 12-step program say, "Hand it over to God." I thought that was a cop-out, and that they were suggesting I sit back in my lazy chair rather than address my problems. I believed that I, and no one else, was in control of my life (and a few other people's lives while I was at it). I was my own God. And that is far too much pressure for anyone, especially a single mom going through divorce.

I continued to believe I was in charge and in control of my life, my work destiny, and occasionally other people's lives until I buckled under the pressure. In the winter of 2011, my business started faltering, my mom was diagnosed with cancer, I didn't have any publishing prospects for my book, and I found myself making the same mistakes with my new partner as I had with Jeremy. I felt overwhelmed and terrified. "I can't do this," I cried one night to myself. "I need help." I thought about calling a friend or my therapist, but wanted more help than that. I didn't know exactly what kind of help I needed; I just knew I needed more than someone listening. So I prayed for the first time in my life. "Please help me," I said. "I can't do this on my own." I didn't know who or what I was praying to, I just knew that trying harder and harder to fix my problems wasn't getting me anywhere. I needed to hand things over and let go.

I still wrestled with the Higher Power notion, but reading and rereading Melody Beattie's *Language of Letting Go* helped me accept my vague notions. "The more we thank God for who God is, who we are, and the exact nature of our present circumstances, the more God acts in our behalf... how I come to understand God is not nearly as important as knowing that God understands me."

I took these words to mean that I didn't necessarily need to understand who or what this Higher Power was. I just needed to understand it wasn't me. I also needed to accept my current situation and myself for what it was and who I was, not what I wanted it to be. Being able to hand things over at times—even if I didn't understand whom or what I was handing them over to—changed my life dramatically. Repeatedly recognizing that things worked out for the best when I didn't try to control or manage them helped letting go become easier. It also allowed me to feel less alone with my struggles and accomplishments because I wasn't trying to manage them all alone. This isn't to say I stopped addressing my issues, hopes, or problems. I just learned how to gauge when I had done enough and it was time to let go and trust that someone or something could take it from there.

CHAPTER 10

FINANCIAL CONCERNS

COUNTLESS WOMEN HAVE ADMITTED TO ME, "I'd love to get divorced, but I can't afford it." Ironically, these women were usually affluent. "*Who Needs Marriage? A Changing Institution,*" a recent *Time Magazine* article, explained it this way: "In recent years, the overall rate of divorce has plateaued somewhat, and leaving a spouse is on the decline among college graduates. But that drop is being offset by a rise in splits among those at the lower end of the socioeconomic spectrum, the people least able to afford to divorce, so the rate is still high."

This study validates my opinion that when women feel as if they can't emotionally afford to stay married, they'll stop letting finances be a barrier. This isn't to say finances shouldn't be considered when deciding to separate, but you shouldn't immediately think you can't support yourself financially before you explore all your options.

Understand Your Finances

Before you put your house on the market or even trade your car in for a bicycle, get a clear understanding of your finances. Your financial situation is probably in flux and may not be crystal clear for you at this moment, but it's still important to grasp it as much as you can. Budget counselor Judy Lawrence is quoted in *The Divorce Recovery Sourcebook* as saying, "Organizing your financial life is also tremendously empowering. It allows you to be proactive about your money, rather than reacting when the bills come in. You will be able to see your choices about how you can make your financial life workable."

Alimony

If you receive alimony, view it as a temporary grace period, because that's what it is. Usually, alimony agreements are for a finite period. This means at some point, you will need to find another way to supplement your income. Lucky for you, you don't have to do this while also filing for divorce. But you still need to do it.

Make a plan for yourself and start taking steps towards it. If the new career you desire requires you to go back to school, budget for that while you are receiving alimony. Remember that returning to school not only takes several years from the application process to graduation, it also takes time every day. Budget and plan for how this will impact your work schedule. And please don't think you can work full-time, go to school full-time, take care of your children, and recover from a divorce all at the same time. Be realistic and gentle with yourself. Sure, pursue your dreams, but do so in a sustainable, sane way. By focusing on one or two goals at a time, you are more likely to be able to achieve them. You can always tackle goals three and four after you've achieved your first two.

Sharing Your Home as a Way to Reduce Expenses

I didn't receive alimony or child support, so I needed to reduce my expenditures immediately. Both Jeremy and I agreed that we would like to keep the house for the kids' sake for at least a year, if possible. Although selling the house would have given both of us a nice nest egg to buffer us for a while, it was a huge relief to not sell. I loved my house. The kids were both born in the bedroom they now shared and had lived in the house for their entire lives. Their placentas were buried in the front yard under trees I'd planted for them. To say I had a deep connection to my house is an understatement.

My house was more than a house for me; it was my refuge. Selling the house would have caused another huge change and disruption in our lives—just when we needed stability the most. Marriage and family therapist Tanya Valenti says, "If at all possible, try to not have more than one large change a year. Kids can handle one change, such as you and your partner separating. Two changes, such as moving homes or changing schools, will be more stressful to them and could delay their healing and adjustment to the divorce."

Once I knew we weren't going to move, I considered having someone live with us to help pay the mortgage. I was nervous about this idea because I loved my alone time, and with Jeremy gone I was able to make the house truly mine. It reflected me and my kids, and I didn't want to jeopardize that or start to feel uneasy in my own house. I reminded myself that compromises were coming, and that having a roommate was a far better option than selling the house and moving into an apartment.

A year earlier, we had transformed our basement from a cold, cement floor junk pile to a cozy spare bedroom and large play room for the kids. It had its own entrance, its own bathroom, and a door that locked. The kids were not particularly attached to it, seeing as it was not within my sight. They were still young enough to want to play near me and didn't really need their own space. Plus, with spring on its way, they were more likely to play outside than they were downstairs.

The space would allow a renter to have her own living space and we would have to share only the kitchen. I decided I could live with that, and on a whim asked our babysitter Jenn if she would ever want to live with us. "I would love to live with you guys!" was her response.

"Really? You wouldn't mind all of the noise from the kids?"

"No, I can sleep through anything."

She was the ideal roommate for me because I already knew her and trusted her. I asked her what her current rent was and offered her our downstairs for the same price, reducing it if she exchanged childcare for part of the rent. She did. I never drafted up a lease or agreement, because I trusted her and was new to being a landlord. With subsequent roommates, I drafted leases and chose the rental price based on actual research, not a whim.

We agreed to try it out month-to-month, and Jenn moved in a month later. She ended up staying with us for over three years and provided so much more than money. She gave us a sense of being a family and was another adult the kids could talk to and trust. The first time I met her, I said, "It feels like you're my sister." She nodded, understanding the connection, and that connection grew while she lived with us.

Living with Jenn provided me with several phases of healing. By paying a third of my mortgage and watching my kids, I had the opportunity not only to stay with my writing career but also to grow my editing business. She was home just enough to combat some of the loneliness I felt at times, but she was independent enough that I could be by myself with my own thoughts. And she provided an additional loving presence in our house during a time when we needed that the most. An added surprise: I actually sought her counsel when I started dating.

I hadn't had a roommate in over twenty years, so I had no idea that finding one would be so easy and that sharing my home could be so nurturing and beneficial. Even if you don't have a babysitter like Jenn, know that many divorced or single women are probably open to sharing a home. A recent AARP report was cited in *He's History, You're Not*, as stating that more than a third of the 1,200-plus women forty-five and older surveyed said they'd be interested in sharing a house with friends or other women, as long as it included private space. The key is to know what you're looking for in a roommate and shared living arrangement.

FRIENDS ARE NOT ALWAYS THE BEST ROOMMATES

Not all roommate situations are ideal, so take some time to think about it before soliciting a roommate. In general, separating from her partner can make a woman feel unsettled, and she may try to make decisions quickly and without her long-term interests in mind. Sue did exactly that when she invited another single mom to move into her home. She thought it would be great company and a way to share childcare and expenses. The two women had been friends for years, giving Sue the false notion that they would make great roommates. Instead, it cost them their friendship. The roommate responded to her recent separation by going out a lot, which made her an erratic childcare provider. Even when she was home and on duty with the kids, she was often distracted by her phone, looking for the latest text from the latest man. Even worse: after each relationship ended, she slipped into a huge depression.

Sue spoke to the roommate several times and shared her concern about her depression and erratic moods and the effect it had on her kids. Each time, the roommate claimed she would settle down. But then another man would ask her out, and the roller coaster would begin again. Eventually, Sue asked her to move out. This didn't go over well, and the roommate slandered Sue to several of their mutual friends, calling her an "uptight bitch and control freak." For Sue, having a roommate cost her more than it helped her.

Before asking Jenn to move in, I asked my friend Cedar if she and her daughter wanted to move in.

"We'd kill each other," she said. "And no offense, but I need my own kitchen. You and I are too controlling to live with one another."

I wasn't offended. I was grateful to have such an honest and wise friend. Considering your perhaps transitional state, be extra careful and take your time sharing your home with someone. Try to find a roommate through friends, coworkers, or relatives first. Again, I caution inviting a close friend to move in with you, because that could certainly strain if not ruin the friendship. But an acquaintance or friend of a friend is more likely than a stranger to have similar values and tastes.

KNOW WHAT YOU WANT IN A ROOMMATE

If this method doesn't result in any viable candidates and you're forced to post an ad publicly, never disclose that you are a single woman living alone (or with kids). I am embarrassed to admit that I made this mistake. When I told my boyfriend at the time about the deluge of emails that followed mere minutes after my ad was placed, he said, "Do you ever watch the news?" Knowing the answer was no, he informed me, both verbally and with emails containing links to news stories, about women and men being raped, murdered, and otherwise harmed by supposedly normal people responding to their ads on Craigslist. If you post your ad on a public domain such as

Craigslist or even Facebook, don't advertise your status as a single woman living alone. Describe the room and its amenities, the rent, and that it's a shared living situation with kids—but don't announce that you're single. When people respond to the ad and want to view the room, make sure you have someone with you when you show it.

Take the time to ask the candidates as many questions as you want. Remember, you're interviewing each other. You're opening your home to someone. You want to make sure the ground rules, protocols, and nature of the relationship are clear and understood by both parties. Are you merely a landlord or do you want a cooperative living situation? How do you feel about noise? Visitors? Extra vehicles being parked in your driveway? How clean should your roommate be? How much access will they have to your house? Ask yourself all of these questions and more so you can be prepared when they come to view the room.

My friend Cindy rented several rooms in her house for years. "I've done background checks, leases, and called references, but what it really boils down to is my intuition. I've taken in roommates with great references and credit even though my gut felt funny. And you know what, I always regretted it. Conversely, I've taken in people who were in between jobs when my intuition told me it would be fine, and it was."

I am a firm believer in trusting my intuition, and I wholeheartedly support what Cindy said. But for recently divorced women who have never rented their space before, protect yourself with a few back-up methods as well. Bring a trusted friend around to meet the potential roommate or talk with a nonbiased friend about the candidate. Don't assume you and your potential roommate are on the same page; take the time to explain out loud and in terms of a lease what you're looking for and what you're not looking for. Listen to their needs as well and be honest with yourself if their needs work for you.

I had a darling woman straight from the Peace Corps come look at my space. I was so caught up in how she was going to teach the kids and me Spanish and inspire me to ride my bike more and drive less, I glossed over the fact that she was hoping I would build a kitchen downstairs for her. "Sure, that could work," I said. A few days later, memories of how stressful my last remodel was brought me back to reality. With reluctance, I told the darling Peace Corps woman that I couldn't emotionally or financially take on a remodeling project at this time.

Working More/Changing Jobs

Here's a hard truth: your life is going to change, and it may not always feel as if it's for the better. Most women I know learned to live more simply when they divorced. They didn't go on vacation for a few years, gave up extras such as gym memberships and after-school activities, and in general rearranged their priorities. They also increased their work schedule or changed jobs to one that was more lucrative.

But here's the good news. Those statistics that say women's earning potential decreases thirty-five percent after they divorce, compared to men's income, which increases twenty-five percent, have recently been proven wrong. "The Pew Economic Mobility Project, an initiative of The Pew Charitable Trust, finds 20 percent of women are going to see gains of more than 25 percent in income after a divorce—double what it was 20 years ago. Men only have a 16 percent gain after a divorce, according to the survey."[12]

Wendy is proof of this study. Within a year of separating from her husband, she tripled her income and bought the house from him. After he moved out, she was wooed by a Fortune 500 company that offered over three times what she was currently earning, not to mention stock options and bonuses. Her main concern was her son and if her job would require too much time away from him. The company worked with her on a schedule that allowed her to be there for her son in the evenings and drop him off at daycare in the morning. Once that was agreed upon, she accepted the job. Being the wise woman she was, even before starting the new job, she met with a financial planner to invest half of her income before it ever entered her bank account. "I'm used to living on far less and don't want to get trapped in this job if I don't like it just because I've acquired expensive tastes," Wendy said. She had seen too many friends become trapped in jobs they didn't like because they lived beyond their means. She was determined not to let that happen to her.

Most women I know feared the negative impact a job change or increase in hours would have on their children. It's a valid concern. It is difficult, but not impossible, to follow Tanya's advice and minimize the changes we make in the first year after separating. My son loathed babysitters, so I did all I could to not inflict them upon him. While still married, I worked at night once Jeremy got home, wrote while my son napped, and even brought him to the classes I taught for the first two years of his life.

For a year after separating from Jeremy, I taught, saw clients, and wrote from 9:00-2:30 four days a week, the hours the kids were in school. I looked over student papers, edited clients' work, and completed any freelance work I had from 8:00 at night to midnight, while the kids slept. I was lucky to have the flexibility to do so, but eventually it became too choppy and exhausting. The kids were going to have to deal with a babysitter.

My friend Rose, a single mother, continued to piecemeal her income through bookkeeping jobs and being a personal chef in order to be home for her daughter before and after school. After years of financial stress, she decided to go back to school to become an accountant. The primary allure was the steady paycheck. Unfortunately, this did mean less time with her daughter, but Rose felt confident in her choice because her daughter had had five years to adjust to her parents being separated before Rose made this change.

In *The Divorce Recovery Sourcebook*, career counselor Kathy Potter claims the changes that occur during a divorce often trigger a desire to change one's career. "Divorce forces most people into some self-assessment... Knowledge, especially about who we are and how we interact, is power." She advises women to pursue their financial and career dreams after their divorce, but to do it slowly, as Rose did. Making a drastic career change during your divorce is not advisable. Stabilize your life as much as you can for yourself and your children, and then with time and insight, start to move your career and finances in a way that better suits you.

CHAPTER 11

YOUR BODY

Reacquainting Yourself With Your Body

YOU PAINTED YOUR BEDROOM a luscious eggplant color. You've taken a good look at your finances and figured out how you can make it through the next few months or maybe even year. You've reached out to other divorced women. You've taken some time to be by yourself and cry, rage, mourn, and consider your part in the divorce. Now, it's time to take a look at your body.

"What?!" you say.

That's right lady, time to take it off. You've been looking at your emotional state, now it's time to look at your physical state. I'm guessing I'm not the only one who's had the occasional affair with a pound cake. There's nothing wrong with that, I love a good treat. It's only a problem if the chocolate bar became your way to cope, and way to not cope. When that happens, you're no longer treating yourself, you're ignoring reality.

Speaking of ignoring things, when is the last time you looked at your naked body? If you can't remember, we're in trouble. When you took a gander, did you groan or smile? Or was it all a blur because you were running so fast to put on your natty old bathrobe? Don't worry, I won't make you get rid of said bathrobe, but I will encourage you to stop hiding behind it.

Be Kind When Looking at Yourself

The first thing to remember when reacquainting yourself with your long-lost friend — which is you in the flesh — is that she's aged. Do not expect her to look twenty when she's forty. Be kind to her. Remember all that she has done for you. Perhaps she carried and birthed a few babies for you. Maybe she's climbed mountains, pedaled bikes, or stayed in downward dog for way longer than she wanted to. Even if she hasn't done any of these things in a long time — or ever — she has carried groceries for you, walked miles (even if it was just from the car to the office door) and cleaned your bathroom for you. And for that, she deserves credit and respect.

Another good thing to remember is that every woman (at least that I know) is dissatisfied with at least one aspect of her body. One woman thinks her nose is too big, another that her breasts are too small, another her butt is too wide, or hair is too curly. Perhaps it's not a specific area you are disgruntled with, but more of an overall desire to be more firm, smooth, thin, or voluptuous. No one is perfect, because we aren't supposed to be. That goes for our emotional state as well as our physical appearance.

Sheila Ellison in her book, *The Courage to Love Again*, claims, "Once we think about ourselves as sensual, creative, and powerful women, the next step is to begin to honor our bodies." She suggests creating a new set of personal beliefs as a way to honor ourselves. One of her personal beliefs is, "Every part of my body is beautiful and clean. I will not be ashamed, and I will make no excuses for imperfections."

If creating a new set of personal beliefs about yourself and your body doesn't appeal to you, that's fine. But I invite you to try, even if it is just for thirty seconds, to focus on an area of your body that you do like. Maybe it's your hair, or your legs, or your smile, or your elbow. I don't care what it is or if it's even visible for most people, I just want you to appreciate at least one area of your body. Good, that's progress. We'll work on the least favorite areas later.

Everyone has Aged, not Just You

I considered my body while getting divorced about as much as I thought about the mating habits of tarantulas. I was so wrapped up in my emotions I didn't care about my body. This isn't to say I ate nothing but pizza for months straight. I still walked every day and ate well-balanced meals, along with my lover, the pound cake. I didn't abuse my body, I just didn't think about it. About five seconds after Jeremy moved out, people asked me when I was going to start dating again. My response was usually, "Never," but their questions started seeping into my self-conscious. "Dating?" I thought. "I vaguely remember that term. I think it involved the opposite sex."

!

For a month or two, the term "opposite sex" frightened me so much I couldn't process anymore. "Don't worry, pound cake! I'm still here for you!" I'd call out. And back to my lover's arms I went.

Time passed and I dared to go a little bit further with this dating notion. "Yes, dating would involve talking to men," I told myself.

!

"Steady now girl, you can do this. Maybe some day you could have coffee with a man. That wouldn't be too bad, would it?"

!

Just as I was running to the store to find another pound cake, a friend invited me out for margaritas and tacos. She had very recently separated from her husband, but was already dating. This alone shocked and horrified me. She terrorized me further by joyfully announcing she went skinny dipping with a man on the second date.

I spit taco all over her as I screamed, "Oh my God, are you insane?" I'm no prude. I worked at a "clothing optional" facility in my youth and still enjoyed being naked. When I was by myself! But with a man I didn't know in broad daylight? Hell no! Suddenly, being nervous about having coffee with a man seemed laughable. Now, dating a man meant getting naked.

No man except my ex-husband had seen my naked body in nearly fifteen years. We all know husbands stop being considered "men" after about five years. Walking around naked in front of Jeremy felt like walking around by myself: neither of us noticed my nudity anymore. It wasn't that he didn't find me attractive; he was very good about telling me I looked nice. But that was always when we were dressed up to go out. Naked wasn't sexy for us, it was real life. I was naked while giving birth to both of our children. I was naked while vomiting with the flu. I was naked while getting out of the bath. I was not naked, doing a strip tease, while offering endless blow jobs. I was naked and sitting on the toilet. And unless that's your fetish, toilet naked is not sexy.

"You let him see you naked in broad daylight?" I asked my brazen friend.

"Sure," she said.

"Weren't you scared?"

"No," she laughed.

She ordered another glass of wine; I changed my order from a water to another margarita, and braced myself for the horrendous details. She and her date left work early on a sunny day, which Seattleites view as holidays, and met at a secluded spot on Lake Washington. They chatted for a few minutes, stripped off their clothes, and dove in the water. I gasped and shouted, "No way!" so many times, all of the other patrons around us were not only privy to our conversation, they were hanging on her every word.

"You are a rock star!" I said as I high-fived her. "I can't believe you stripped in front of a man you hardly know. And that you felt good about it!"

"It's not as if any of us have great bodies anymore. I've got stretch marks and a saggy tummy from babies. He has an extra fifteen pounds or so in his gut and man boobs. But we're still attracted to one another. In fact, the sex was hot!"

The entire restaurant went silent as they listened for the details, which they heard. But I'm sorry, you'll have to wait. This chapter is just about your body. We'll get to sex in the next chapter.

Although horrifying, my friend's story helped me. I knew my body had changed over the years, but somehow failed to realize that everyone else's bodies had changed as well. I had no idea what people my age looked like. The last time I had been naked around people who weren't my husband or children, I was twenty years old. It was time to do some research. I still wasn't ready to show my naked body to a man, but I was ready to look at it myself and other middle-aged naked bodies.

Look at Other Bodies

It so happened that one of my favorite alone-time activities involved naked bodies. The Korean Spa, what I dubbed the "naked lady spa," had provided me with camaraderie and peace on many Saturday nights. I now added "check out other bodies" as part of my spa agenda. I loved the days the spa was full of European women, because with them, I didn't have to be sly about staring. I stared at their boobs, they stared at mine. I checked out their bellies, they looked at my butt. Then we smiled at one another and went our separate ways.

What I learned from my investigation was: my boobs weren't the tiniest boobs on the planet, which I had been convinced was true. My butt held up pretty well over the years, but was probably going to disappoint me any day now. Large women were often more confident than skinny women. Old women got Brazilian waxes. When noticing this I made a note to myself: the seventies are over, time for some personal grooming to my bikini area. No one looked good wearing a pink hair net (along with being naked, wearing the hairnet was mandatory at the spa). Good posture could make all the difference. When women were young and beautiful, they often wasted it being self-conscious and insecure. Confident middle-aged women were gorgeous. Old women didn't care about this crap anymore. I looked forward to being one of them.

But the biggest lesson of all was that bodies varied in every way imaginable and were only a small aspect of what made the women attractive. Her smile and the way she held herself affected her attractiveness more (with and without clothes). When her inner confidence and warmth radiated outwards, it was all I could do to not return that with a smile or by striking up a conversation. Being approachable made people very attractive. I expanded my study to include men (clothed obviously) and the general public and noticed who I felt drawn to was almost always based on their openness.

Emotional Changes Cause Physical Changes

Although I was still not willing to date, something must have been shifting in me internally, because men started talking to me. I received catcalls and whistles for the first time in years; men struck up conversations while waiting in line; and some even asked for my phone number. Amy Botwinick, in *Congratulations on Your Divorce,* shares a similar experience. Although she was exhausted and frazzled she says, "I was probably more attractive because of my new-found self confidence. For years, my self-esteem was in the toilet and I was very unhappy. Making a choice to divorce and finally telling the world was like putting down a ten-pound bag of bullshit."

My friend Jill described the newfound interest men seemed to have in us as "the light being turned on." By the time my daughter was two years old, I knew my marriage was in trouble. I was often tired, stressed, or distracted. I didn't radiate. I didn't capture people's attention. My light was definitely not on. Although I spent a good portion of that year in "man land"—paint supply stores, plumbing stores, and Home Depot—I don't remember one man flirting with me or even initiating a conversation. I felt invisible.

A year later, I separated from Jeremy and started hanging out with naked women. Although I was still deeply mourning the end of my marriage, some of my light must have been turned back on. Ashton Applewhite in her book, *Cutting Loose: Why Women Who End Their Marriages Do So Well,* claims, "A change in outward behavior is often the first sign of an inner change that is just beginning to make itself known." Although I didn't know it yet, the men could sense that my light and confidence were returning. I was far from being ready to date, but I did enjoy the one-minute exchange with a man on the street. It was just enough to boost my confidence and make me realize I was no longer invisible.

It's All Right to Spend Money on Your Body

Once other people started to notice me, I had to notice myself. And once I did, I had to admit that part of feeling invisible was due to *trying* to be invisible. I'd been hiding behind baggy, paint-spattered, blueberry-stained clothes since my kids were born. I didn't enjoy shopping, and going on a shopping spree downtown was not in my budget. But with the encouragement of some friends who did enjoy shopping, I started scouring consignment shops and thrift stores for fun clothes. It took a while, but I am proud to say I developed the gift of thrifting. But some things you can't, or shouldn't, buy at thrift stores, such as lingerie.

"Lingerie?" you ask, "what's that?"

And I was right with you on that one. I was married, why did I need lingerie? I barely had a decent bra, I certainly didn't have any crotchless panties. That is until a somewhat bossy, but ever dear friend screamed in horror when she saw the bandana like structure I called a bra.

"What the hell is that?" she asked.

"A bra."

"That is not a bra. Bras are pretty and lacy. They make you feel good. That… that, well I don't know what that is."

"Please," I said. "It's not as if I even need a bra. I only wear this to hide my THO (titty hard ons)."

"THOs are sexy, no need to hide them. But wear a bra when you want a little more umph. A little va-va-voom."

I laughed, knowing my barely A cups were never going to be va-va-voom.

"Look at me," my skinny, small-chested friend said as she lifted her shirt. And damn if she wasn't right. She had cleavage! And a beautiful lacy thing was helping create that cleavage. "See," she said pulling her shirt back down and sticking out her chest. "I have boobs! Or at least I look like I do." She taught me all about the wonders of bras that day. Bras that lift and support, even when you think there's nothing to lift. Bras that come with gel packs inside to increase your cup size. And bras that are pretty and feel good to put on. I gasped when she told me the price of such items, but went shopping with her anyway. And she was right, they were worth every penny.

Amy Botwinick says, "You are a completely different person now, and it's time for you to show it on the outside too. Take your self-esteem up another notch by improving your appearance with something as simple as a new hairstyle or new wardrobe. How you feel on the inside is most important, but feeling good about how you look can give you the extra confidence and zip in your step."

After my friend Wendy changed jobs and tripled her income shortly after her divorce, a benevolent, yet discerning friend, told her, "If you want to be successful, you need to dress successful." He said her previously considered work clothes were fine for lounging around the house, but it was time to buy some real clothes. "And I never want to see those again," he screamed while pointing at her Birkenstocks.

A new pair of glasses, pair of jeans, two pairs of boots and a few blouses cost Wendy what she used to make in a month. She returned home a bit shell-shocked and definitely pale, but by the end of the night was parading around in her new boots and sexy yet sophisticated blouse. Months later she claimed the clothes were the best thing she could have done for herself. "Every time I wear them I remember how far I've come and that I'm a success, not a failure."

I know many women who replaced their entire wardrobe after their divorce or spent an exorbitant amount on cosmetics and face creams, all of which I support. I even support a woman I know who got a tummy tuck. No amount of Pilates or crunches reduced the bulge she had from carrying very large twins. A doctor explained that her abdomen wall separated while the twins were in utero and she "could do crunches day and night, but it wasn't going to give her a flat stomach."

"It's not as if I expect it to be flat, it wasn't even flat when I was twenty," she said. "I just want it to look like it did before I had kids."

Although plastic surgery is an extreme way to improve her appearance, I believe it's a woman's right to decide to do so. Follow Amy Botwinick's advice: "I'm all for plastic surgery and doing things that can improve your appearance; however, the beauty you feel inside has to match the outside beauty. Most people will tell you that the most attractive quality a person can have is confidence. That comes with a healthy self-esteem which needs constant tweaking and a spirit and soul that needs constant nourishment."

If you choose to alter your external appearance as well, be sure you are doing it for yourself, not as a way to "get a man" or as a way to avoid exercising. I'm all for self-improvement as long as it's for yourself, not because someone is telling you that you need it, and isn't followed by a stream of self-criticism and deprecation. There may be areas you choose to change because you have the means to, which is great, but please do so with love. Don't ridicule or despise your body, it's done a lot for you.

Getting in Physical Shape

Sophie, a thirty-seven-year-old graphic designer, claimed she wanted to lose ten pounds before she started dating. All of her friends said, "You don't need to do that. You look great the way you are."

"I know I'm not horribly overweight," she said. "But I also know I can look better. I used to work out all the time, but got too distracted with the divorce. I'm doing it for me, so I can feel better about myself."

Sophie's friends were doing what friends do, which is support one another. They wanted Sophie to feel good about herself, so originally told her she looked great, because she did. But once they heard about Sophie's plan to start training for a 10K and start lifting weights again because she *missed* it, they supported her in her new goals. Exercising is a great way to burn off some of the excess stress and adrenaline that accompanies divorce. It also allows you to start noticing and hopefully appreciating your body again.

Ashton Applewhite describes getting physically in shape as analogous to seeing a therapist for mental health; both are ways to take care of yourself. She claims that by looking and feeling better, it is easier for women to envision a different, better future for themselves after divorce. "Taking care of one's body is a part of taking responsibility for oneself, and it's an important component in building self-esteem."

Even if you choose to get in shape for vanity reasons, I support that. Getting divorced is tremendously hard on the ego. Exercising, eating right, weight training, and enrolling in fitness classes, can all help a woman feel better about herself. By spending time and money on herself, she is starting to value herself again. As long as the new exercise regime is approached with patience and pride, not shame, it should be beneficial both physically and emotionally.

I enrolled in yoga classes as a way to relieve stress and strengthen my upper body. I accomplished that and my arm muscles became more defined than they had ever been. I celebrated on the day I could do a series of sun salutations without buckling. "Wow, I'm a yoga star!" I congratulated myself while holding plank pose. But an added bonus of the class was the other women I met, who became friends. And the best gift of all was how the breathing techniques, which I dismissed in the beginning because I thought they were a waste of time, proved to be valuable coping mechanisms when stuck in traffic, fighting insomnia, and they even helped me through several painful medical procedures. The combination of the physical and mental improvements made my yoga class one of the best gifts I ever gave myself.

Hopefully, we can all get to a place where we thank our bodies and appreciate them for what they are. I know with media's influence and society's worship of young and thin, not every woman is going to parade her naked self proudly. And that's all right. Parading naked isn't for everyone. But my hope is that if you've been avoiding the mirror, scowl whenever you see yourself, or cringe at the idea of anyone seeing any part of your body, that at least some of that will change for you. Start with a pedicure if you like. There's no need to run a marathon or buy out Macy's. A $20 pedicure can be just the gift you need for yourself. And no one even needs to see your hot red toenails, but you'll know they're there. And when you think of them, I hope you smile and compliment them on their beauty.

CHAPTER 12

DATING

ADVICE ON WHEN TO START DATING AGAIN after your divorce often involves complicated algorithms involving how many years you were married, divided by how many years you were unhappy, times the square root of 2343 and…well, I lost track after the first division. Some friends started dating as soon as they separated from their ex. Others refused to go on a date or return a man's call even six years after their divorce. Sue would date several men for months and then take five months for herself without sexual relations or dates. Each woman's timeline worked for her, and the timelines were rarely linear.

Start with Dating—Just Dating

Going on a date means spending an hour or so with a man, not marrying him. Possibly, the last man you dated ended up being your husband, but that does not have to be your goal this time around. If the thought of remarrying turns your stomach, rest assured that you are not alone. Statistics from the US Census Bureau show that the percentage of women remarrying within five years of their divorce has been steadily decreasing since 1955.[9] If you are not one of the queasy ones and are instead someone who wants to forego the hassles of dating and head directly to the altar, please remember this: In 2006, the U.S. Census Bureau found that 60 percent of second marriages and 73 percent of third marriages end in divorce.[13]

Even if you've followed all of my advice and have taken time to grieve, be alone, and appreciate your body, this only prepares you for *dating*. The good news is, dating prepares you for your next *relationship*. Dating is a necessary part of learning how to trust again. I'm not necessarily referring to trusting men. I'm talking about trusting yourself. Having faith and trust in yourself is a crucial step to healing and moving on.

If considerable time has passed since your separation and you still don't want to date, ask yourself why. Are you still hanging on to anger and resentment? Those emotions may be protecting you, but they're also hurting you. Plus, they're lousy lovers, remember? Maybe it's time to let the negativity go and let some kindness, acceptance, and love in instead? Not necessarily love of another, but love of *you*, which will radiate out as warmth to others. Even if you don't want to date, I still encourage you to occasionally leave the bunny slippers at home and expand your social circle. Although it may feel uneasy at first, eventually it will build your confidence and trust in yourself.

Start Socializing More

The more I was away from my house, the more comfortable I became interacting with other adults I didn't know. Happy Hour was one of my favorite ways to socialize. It was easy to convince my mom friends to join me, because we could eat cheap food while catching up with one another and relinquishing our cooking and other responsibilities for the night. We usually shared a babysitter, so the entire evening often cost less than $40. The best bonus: I was usually home by 9:00 so I wasn't dragging my butt the next day while with my kids.

Another fun way to get my ya-yas out was dancing with my girlfriends. We found a couple dive bars that had 80s nights. Along with other middle-aged people, we could belt out New Order songs and release our inner divas for the night. The fact that the dance floor was often occupied with men in sequins who were willing to twirl us around all night only increased the fun. If bars and dancing aren't your thing, that's fine. Instead, invite a friend out for tea or to go for a walk. I spent many more nights socializing with a friend on her couch than I did singing Madonna songs in dive bars, but I made myself shake my booty occasionally because it was out of my comfort zone, and I was ready to challenge myself in this way.

Other options are attending gallery openings, the theater, or book readings. Or join a class, a book club, or a sports team. Book readings and gallery openings were free activities that didn't require me to hire a babysitter, so I indulged in them frequently. They were also activities I felt comfortable attending on my own. If you need a friend to join you, that's fine, ask one. Let your preferences drive your choices, but be willing to explore new areas of interest as well. Even if you are limited financially or by living in a small town, you still have access to readings at your library and community events. The reading or play held at your local high school may not be your favorite, but the quality of the performance is secondary to you learning how to socialize without your husband. This is the time to learn about yourself and your interests and stretch yourself socially.

A Date Can Mean Many Things

Once you start to feel more comfortable out and about with other adults, your trepidation about dating may lessen. If alarm bells just went off in your head, let me reassure you that a "date" can mean many things. Dr. Robert Albert says in *After Your Divorce: Creating the Good Life on Your Own,* that people date for a variety of reasons, including looking for companionship without a commitment, stimulating conversation, the excitement that goes along with flirting and attraction, or sexual gratification. He also advises dating when you're ready; not because your friends want you to. Take some time to ask yourself what you are ready for, what you want, and what you need at this point in your healing process. Equally important is asking yourself what you're *not* ready for. Ask yourself what you feel is lacking in your life and what you feel ready for. Maybe you long for a man's attention, but hyperventilate at the thought of kissing someone. That's fine, ask a man to see a movie with you. It doesn't need to lead anywhere else until you're ready. As long as you're honest with yourself and the people you're interacting with, you are operating with integrity.

People date as a way to relieve boredom, to stroke their ego, to experience people and activities out of their normal social circle, to have sex, to be held, to flirt, to alleviate loneliness, to help them get over an ex, and a host of other reasons. Dating isn't charity work, so don't judge yourself if your reasons for doing so seem shallow. Dating also doesn't need to mean anything or lead to anything. It can just be something you do because you're tired of your own company. Don't judge yourself for your reasons, but don't lie to yourself either. Admit to yourself—without shame—what drives your need so you can be honest with the people you date. It's only a problem if you're dishonest with the person you're dating and lead him on. If you tell him, "I'm only available for casual dating at this time," or "I'm still getting over my ex," he has the information he needs to decide whether or not that is acceptable for him. There's no right or wrong way to begin dating again. But it will feel wrong to you and the people you date if you are unclear about what your intentions are.

Remember How to Flirt

Expanding my social circles and being willing to socialize outside of my house eventually led to flirting. Remembering how to flirt was like riding a bicycle. It came back to me quickly, but I was a little wobbly and awkward at first. But once I got used to it again, it became second nature.

A man tried to engage my friends and me in conversation one night when we were out for dinner. They turned their backs on him and said, "We're all married." I piped up, "I'm not," and grinned at him. I wasn't ready to date at this time, but I was ready to engage with men, and this man was very engaging. He was a beautiful African-American man with a hearty laugh and bold personality. He stood out like an orchid compared to the withdrawn men in the restaurant who were transfixed by their iPhones. I talked and laughed with Mr. Dark and Charismatic for a few minutes and then returned my attention to my friends. "Wow," Mary said. "I have totally forgotten how to do that."

"No you haven't," I said. "You're just out of practice."

In my opinion, all flirting is, is focusing my attention on a person I am attracted to. Sometimes it means laughing a lot and sometimes it's holding eye contact and listening intently. Other times, I tease a person as a way to be flirtatious or touch their arm when I'm talking, but often it's subtler than that. You know your comfort level with physical touch and communication style, so let that dictate how you communicate with people you are attracted to.

If you have doubts about your flirting ability, rest assured that often all it takes is smiling at someone. Dr. Linda Papadopoulos, author of *What Men Say, What Women Hear,* claims that "men assume that behavior described by women as 'just being friendly' is actually flirtatious and the other party is 'interested.'" So something as small as smiling at a man or catching his eye is often considered flirting and may be reciprocated.

I watched my non-flirtatious (often married) friends became confident flirters in about an hour. After our encounter with Mr. Charismatic, Mary started flirting with our waiter rather effortlessly and easily. And the next time we went out, she chatted effortlessly with the man in the booth next to us.

"Should I feel guilty?" Mary asked me at one point in the evening.

"Hell no! Dan (her husband) is going to reap the benefits of this because you're going to return home revved up."

"I know," she giggled. "He likes it when I go out with you."

Learning how to flirt again was good for my ego. It helped me learn how to interact with men again, and it was a step towards dating. Sure, being with other single women may have aided my attempts, but I was pleasantly surprised at how willing my married friends joined me. We confessed to their husbands that a little flirting occurred while we were out, but reassured them it would never lead to anything else besides harmless attention. (When one of my married friends wanted to cross this boundary and make out with a man, I said I needed to go home and I hoped she would come with me.)

Hopefully being exposed to more single people will allow you to feel more comfortable talking to people you don't know, but would like to know. If flirting isn't your thing, that's fine, but still try talking to someone new in your book group or to someone you don't know while attending a reading with a friend. This practice will help you immensely when you're ready to start dating again.

All Needs are Acceptable

When I first started dating, my primary need was sexual. I wasn't ready for a relationship, but my hormones were on overdrive, so I opened my mind to the previously horrifying thought of dating. Genevieve Clapp in her book *Divorce and New Beginnings,* says an insatiable appetite for sex after a divorce is common. She also says that many men and women are baffled by their arousal and uncharacteristic behavior, but that in actuality it makes sense because it is a way to bolster sagging self-esteem and prove one's attractiveness and desirability. "Casual partners have the advantage of requiring neither commitment nor trust," she says, "which is appealing to many who still feel vulnerable after divorce."

Surprisingly, it was more difficult than I thought to find a man who was willing to have a no-strings-attached relationship with me. The last time I'd dated, I was twenty-two, and back then, a casual sexual relationship was every man's dream. As I learned over and over again, things had changed during the fourteen years that I was married. I knew a casual relationship was all I was capable of because, as Clapp explained, I was still vulnerable from my divorce. The irony was, several of the men I propositioned claimed they were too vulnerable to ONLY have a casual relationship. They needed to get to know me, build trust, and then maybe, just maybe, have sex. So back to my therapist I went. She kindly explained that men in their forties were complicated and if I wanted a simple, casual (she called it a booty call, which I cringed at, but had to admit was true) relationship, I needed to seek out a younger man.

"How much younger?" I asked.

"In his mid-twenties," she replied.

"No way! What would I have in common with a man that age? He'll talk about keg parties and call me 'dude.'"

I left her office in disbelief. I knew dating would be confusing, which was why I wanted no part of it. But sex? I thought that would be simple and easy. If I believed my therapist, the only way to have uncomplicated sex was 1) to pay for it or 2) to cruise college campuses and 7-11s.

Casual Dating

Lucky for me, an attractive, soulful, funny, and intelligent twenty-six-year-old asked me out several weeks later. No, I didn't meet him at the Slurpee counter. I met him while at a pub with a friend. After laughing and saying, "My therapist told me to do this!" I accepted a date with him. He soon became the casual partner I was looking for.

Although I was hoping to actually meet someone who remembered the 80s—or at least was born in them—and yes, I was occasionally called "dude," the beautiful thing about the young men I met was their forthrightness and exuberance. Compared to men my age, men in their twenties were uninhibited in approaching me first and were abundant with compliments. This was extremely helpful in repairing my damaged ego and lack of confidence. They also didn't tire easily, if you know what I mean. As the authors of *Our Turn: The Good News about Women and Divorce* say, "Physiologically, a woman in her forties and a man in his twenties have similar testosterone levels, which play a large part of desire."

Feel Free to Explore Your Sexual and Physical Desires

Dating casually and dating young men satisfied me for over a year. As I said, it was desire that finally got me out of the house. I wanted to be pressed up against a wall and kissed all over. I wanted to groan with anticipation and experience lust again. Remember making out? I didn't, but I remembered I missed it, and that was enough encouragement to start dating. Knowing I didn't have a future (or past, for that matter) with these men allowed me to be uninhibited in a way I had never been before.

Ashton Applewhite, author of *Cutting Loose: Why Women Who End Their Marriages Do So Well*, says many divorced women experience a sexual revolution. "Leaving a marriage, abandoning the fort, is such a deeply transgressive act that other taboos lose their hold on women who have taken that first bold step. They reject the tired premise that only naughty girls take the sexual initiative, and refuse to stick to the object-of-desire nice girl role; either scenario becomes possible along with the whole spectrum in between."

I had a confidence in myself as a single forty-year-old that I didn't have as a single twenty-year-old or married thirty-six year-old. This translated to being freer and more daring in asking for what I wanted from my partners. I was liberated from the resentments which inhibited sex in my marriage as well as from the confounds of the usual and the norm. Even more important, I stopped judging and inhibiting myself. I learned a lot about what I liked and needed and took that knowledge with me once I was ready to enter a real relationship.

Sheila Ellison, in her book *The Courage to Love Again*, claims that most women's sexual identity becomes bruised after divorce. Maybe they were betrayed or rejected, and therefore doubt their sexual skills and appeal. She says women can help themselves form positive sexual identities by examining where the negative ones came from and begin viewing their bodies as beautiful. She says that "it is hard to heal many of the sexual ideas we have about ourselves on our own. ...Until someone is actually looking at us as we disrobe we won't know if we have the courage to live our new beliefs." She also claims that if we don't work out any past sexual issues or inhibitions with new partners, we will carry these negative beliefs into our next relationship.

As long as it involves two consensual adults, shame should never be a part of sex. Sex should be liberating, rewarding, fun, orgasmic, varied, and as frequent as you like. If your sexual identity has suffered bumps and bruises along the way or even merely felt restricted, this is your time to change that. Once sex becomes something else, it's really hard to get it back to this free and varied state.

Or Don't, If That's Not Your Thing

Some experts, such as Bruce Fisher, marriage and family therapist and author of the *Rebuilding* series, recommend finding alternate ways to meet your needs other than casual affairs. I feel this advice is based on the assumption that women are looking for intimacy and touch rather than sex. Or that they use their sexuality to feel desired, when what they really want is to be complimented, not fornicated. If this is true for you, consider following Fisher's advice and seek other ways to bolster your self-esteem and meet your needs. Call a friend and ask her to compliment you, get a massage, snuggle with your kids while reading to them, hold a friend's hand or even flirt with men, but don't get naked.

Some women admitted to being sexually frustrated after their divorce, but they balked at my suggestion of finding a booty call. "I don't know how to do that," one friend admitted. "Sex always involves an emotional connection for me, yet I'm not ready for a relationship." I complimented her on knowing that about herself and took her shopping for a vibrator. "Better this than getting my feelings hurt," she said when she chose the Rabbit as her gift. She remembered a past booty call she'd had—the man literally had run out of her home in the morning—and how that hurt her feelings. I agreed with her choice. Until she was ready to pursue a relationship with a man, the Rabbit could keep her company.

Where to Meet Men

As I said, the young men I met were usually unabashed in approaching me first. But after a while, I yearned for something more than these young men could offer. I was still awkward at trying to transform interesting conversations at gallery openings into dates, so I asked my friends to introduce me to their single male friends. For me, going out with a friend of a friend was the easiest way to date. I felt comforted knowing that he wasn't a total stranger and we had at least one topic of conversation guaranteed: the mutual friend. It was a gentle, relatively stress-free way to ease into dating.

Friends directly introduced me to men, but they also indirectly did so by getting me off of my couch and away from my lover, the pound cake. As I said before, single people tend to hang out with other single people, so start making friends with single people. Just because they're single doesn't mean they're childless, so if childcare is an issue for you, find parties and events that you can attend with your children. The organization Meetup has groups for everyone, including single parents. They often meet in parks and coffee shops, so no childcare is needed.

I met my first crush at a friend's dinner party. The man worked with my friend as a filmmaker, so I found conversation with him to be scintillating as well as fluid. Small dinner parties were ideal for me because I felt most at ease in small, intimate settings. Unfortunately, interesting dinner parties don't happen every night of the week for me, so I expanded my willingness to meet people in other places. Of course, being in a club, class, or organization with people with similar interests is an ideal place to meet potential dates and friends. I met several interesting men in my yoga classes.

I had a bias against meeting someone at a bar, but I learned through friends that this wasn't as tawdry as it sounded. Obviously if the man was inebriated or spent 50% of his life on a bar stool, I wouldn't chat with him. But I didn't find many of those men in my neighborhood pubs or the places we danced. Most of the patrons were casual drinkers and close to my age. The two men I dated from bars were intelligent, creative, accomplished in their careers, and very kind.

Your workplace may also lend itself to meeting single people. If you don't want to mix your personal life with your work life, that's understandable, but try not to rule out meeting someone through your work connections. They could be only loosely affiliated to your work by working in a building near you. Or they could work with an affiliate company or vendor, or maybe they just know someone you work with. There are many degrees of separation that you could pursue. It's up to you to determine what you feel comfortable with.

Online Dating

Being a Luddite, I was slow to accept online dating as a way to meet men. The idea of staring at a screen as a way to get to know someone baffled me. "I need to know what he looks and sounds like when he laughs. I need to smell him and see if his eyes twinkle before I even consider going on a date with him," I told my friend Susan. "You can't gauge any of that from a computer."

"True, but it allows you access to a ton of men without having to leave your house. And once you agree to meet someone in person, you can sniff him all you want."

I was clearly in the minority, because almost everyone I knew had tried dating online. According to Internet tracking firm Experian Hitwise, collectively the major dating sites had more than 593 million visits in the United States in the month of October, 2011.[14]

I balked and resisted for over a year—to the chagrin of my friends— but eventually I gave in to the lure of online dating. I started with the big one, eHarmony. Until I learned that it was Christian-based and homophobic. I've subsequently heard that this has changed, but at the time they seemed very conservative, so I didn't join. I tried some sites specifically geared for single parents, but the pool wasn't large enough in Seattle for me to meet anyone interesting. I looked at Match.com, but was overwhelmed by a sea of sameness. After Match.com failed me, I tried OK Cupid, the site Susan recommended, and Plenty of Fish (another free site recommended by a friend). I found lots of appealing men on these sites, so I started to write my profile.

CREATING AN ONLINE BIO

Yes, you just heard the screech of brakes. Writing a 300-page novel was easier than writing a 60-word profile. There's a reason successful businesses exist to write your dating profile for you. After agonizing about it for days, I realized I was over-thinking it. It needed to be casual and slightly humorous with just enough information to pique interest. I drank a glass of wine and allowed myself ten minutes to write it. I pushed the send button before I could rephrase every word or even change a comma.

Erica Manfred, author of *He's History, You're Not*, advises that you keep your online profile simple. "Leave out walks on the beach and dining by candlelight. You don't have to list all of your accomplishments, interests, children, or anything else. Just write something short and intriguing about yourself—anything—and leave the details for the first email or phone call."

My bio changed over the years. At first, it was flirty and casual, because that was the kind of dating I was looking for. Once I was ready for a relationship, I revealed more about my spiritual side and the importance of my children. Sometimes I stated a few things I was looking for in a man, like him being intellectually stimulating, and for him to have established the life he wanted for himself. Other times I left that out, figuring I would screen for these things when emailing them. Change your bio as frequently as you like, but follow Manfred's advice and don't necessarily include everything about yourself. That's what the dates are for: to learn about one another. An added bonus of dating was how much I learned about myself and my needs. Those needs changed and expanded, so I left room for that change and growth in my bio.

As for pictures, I steered away from any bikini shots or even pictures that revealed cleavage. Sure, I might have had more responses if I'd included revealing or sexy shots, but not from the kind of man I was looking for. Even when I was looking for a casual relationship, I never admitted that in my bio (or insinuated it by including revealing pictures) because for me, that was just asking to be inundated with undesirable emails.

Susan was right: I met far more men online than I would have met even if I'd gone out every night, which I wasn't willing or able to do. And for the most part, I was glad I dated the men I met even if it was only for a short time. Although I expected it to be awkward to date strangers, the online bios and emails or phone conversations leading up to the date allowed me to feel as if I knew the man. Or at least I had a few topics of interest to discuss by the time we met in person.

Online dating statistics from a survey by *The New York Sunday Times* indicate "that email relationships can be far more intimate than normal dating. Women are most likely to find a potential lover online, with 72% admitting to having had an online romance, compared to 52% of men. The online dating statistics report also found that 33% of all online relationships led to a date."[15]

GO AHEAD AND EMAIL HIM FIRST

At first, I waited for men to contact me through the dating sites. Most of the men who contacted me lived far away or didn't appeal to me, so I changed strategies. I plugged in certain criteria I was looking for and cruised the sites for interesting men. When I found one, I emailed him first.

Feeling free to initiate contact allowed me to have a sense of control. I wasn't sitting by the phone — or the computer in this case — waiting for someone. When I felt like dating, I emailed people. And when I needed a break, I hid my profile or merely stopped initiating contact. Seattle is notorious for its passive men, so it didn't seem overly brazen for me to email men first. The norms in your community may be different, but I highly encourage you to be as bold as you can while Internet dating. I'm not suggesting sending naked photos of yourself or promising lewd sexual acts in your emails. I'm merely suggesting you email as many men as you find interesting. You're safe behind your computer and a made-up screen name; there's no reason to feel ashamed if they don't email you back.

Most men claimed they appreciated that I initiated contact. The key, though, was to eventually back off and let them initiate something. If I emailed them first, then I usually didn't initiate the first face-to-face meeting. This wasn't a rule for me, but rather a guideline. If the man seemed shy, but interested, I went ahead and asked him to coffee first. Trust your intuition on this. You'll know if you don't feel your attention is being reciprocated. If that occurs, back off and see what happens.

Yes, this can sound similar to the dreaded cat and mouse game that I refused to play. But really, playing cat and mouse involves being elusive and unavailable even when you like the man, just so you don't look too available. This is ridiculous. If you like him and he asks you out, don't pretend you have something else to do. Go out with him! But if you've emailed him twice and he hasn't responded, stop emailing him. Or if he takes days to respond, back off again or even stop emailing him altogether. Generally, people who are online are playing the field. If they take a week to get back to you (and don't give a good reason why) it means you are not one of the top people they are pursuing. They're fishing for other fish — which is fine. That's what dating is. But be aware if your efforts are being reciprocated, and if they aren't, move on. There are plenty of people who will put you at the front of their lines.

Know Your Limits

PHYSICAL LIMITS

Dating is a time for you to experiment and explore your needs, not a time to succumb to someone else's wishes. This is especially true if you are experimenting sexually. Make sure that experimentation is dictated by you, that you always feel safe, and that someone else is home with you or knows where you are and is on call if you start to feel uncomfortable. And always trust your intuition. This holds true for any date. If you feel uncomfortable, end the date. Don't worry about his feelings or looking like a tease. A woman has a right to change her mind, say no, and leave whenever she wants.

By not being clear about what they want and don't want, women sometimes compromise their values while in the company of a man, especially when it's a man they are romantically interested in. I've heard tales of women having sex when they really wanted to cuddle, and of women staying out late drinking when they really wanted to have a nice dinner and conversation. One friend almost got literally lost in the woods on a date gone awry. "I knew we were on the wrong trail," Abby explained, "but he kept insisting we weren't lost. I just wanted to go on a gentle three-mile hike along the river, but we ended up scaling boulders and climbing three thousand feet. By the time we finally made it back to the car, it was dark and I had a huge gash on my knee."

Abby was not only frightened and in possible physical danger on her date, she also felt a huge amount of shame and then resentment for not being clearer about her boundaries. This is what we want to avoid at all cost.

Dr. Linda Papadopoulos, author of *What Men Say, What Women Hear*, advises us to state the particular codes of behavior that are important to us *in the beginning of the relationship*. "Even though the first date is where both parties are trying to be on their best behavior, it is also where the boundaries of any potential relationship are set up." She says if you feel strongly about a certain boundary, such as no sex on the first date, be explicit and quick about sharing that.

TIME LIMITS

Be very clear with yourself on how long you want to spend on the date. If you want to spend only an hour on the first date (a time frame I recommend), don't agree to dinner. Instead, propose a coffee date or a short walk. An hour gives you a sense of the man, but isn't so long that you feel held captive. If you enjoy his company, propose spending another hour with him at a later date. I recommend taking time between the first and second date in order to sort out what was reality and what was fantasy.

I left many first dates enthralled with the man. The conversation flowed easily, he appeared charming and intelligent, and I eagerly anticipated the second date. The following day I'd recall how he often interrupted me, or how he was engaging only when the topic involved him. I'd remember some snide comments he'd said about his ex-wife, or how he was rude to the waitress, and suddenly the fabulous date was just an all-right date. This isn't to say I would cancel the second date with him. I probably still agreed to see him again, but I did so with a clearer picture of him, rather than a rose-colored picture.

If it's been a while since you have dated, you may want to follow the same advice. Most marriages end with each partner ignoring and negating the other partner. After years of being negated, it feels good to be paid attention to again. Bask in that attention, but try not to let it skew your perception of the men you date. This can be difficult at first. Over time, your screening factors will become finely tuned, but only if you pay attention to them. Proceed with dating slowly and take time in between dates to sort out who the person is. Determine if you genuinely like and respect him or if you are only drawn to the attention he is giving you.

ACCEPTABLE ACTIVITIES

Along with being clear about the length of the date, be clear about what activities you are comfortable with. For some women, seeing a band or a movie is the ideal date because she can avoid the "What if we don't have anything to talk about?" fear. For others, engaging in a physical activity is most comfortable. And still others might not know because they are out of practice.

I fell into the third category. The first man I dated was twelve years younger than I was. He proposed a hike for our first date. I loved hiking, but quickly learned it was an incredibly awkward way to spend a first date. I was already emotionally very uncomfortable, so being sweaty, out of breath, and otherwise physically challenged didn't help matters. Later, when a different man proposed attending the theater as a first date, I was initially impressed and thrilled to be able to sit while getting to know someone. In actuality, the getting-to-know-him part was greatly restricted because we couldn't talk during the play.

After several more awkward dates, I started suggesting walks or meeting for coffee for first and second dates. I wouldn't say no to any other activity (one man proposed bowling, which was really fun), but I would say no to things that made me uncomfortable or prohibited conversation. Again, ask yourself what you are comfortable with and what you want out of the date. Also, if you're open to it, consider experimenting with what works and doesn't work.

How to End a Date

WHEN YOU'RE NOT INTERESTED

Every date ends with that awkward moment of "what's next?" You can eliminate a lot of this awkwardness if you set limits for yourself ahead of time. If I wasn't interested in the man, I ended the date as early as possible and said, "Thanks for the coffee, I wish you luck." I might shake his hand or even hug him, but I was clear in my mind that this was good-bye. Probably 95% of the time, the man picked up on this, but if he didn't and asked if he could see me again, I said no. If I had a clear reason, such as "the chemistry isn't what I thought it would be" or "we're in different places in our lives," I usually offered it, but a reason isn't mandatory. If the reason was, "I thought you were a total asshole," I kept that to myself and merely wished him good luck in his dating ventures. This isn't an opportunity to insult the man; it's merely a way to make it clear that you're not interested in another date.

"The worst part of dating is the mixed messages," my friend Robert said. "I'd think the date went really well, she'd agree, maybe we'd even kiss a little good night, and then I wouldn't hear back from her. Even if all she texted back was, 'I don't want to go out again,' that would be better than nothing."

This was a common complaint from most of my male friends. Even if you're afraid turning the man down will hurt his feelings, I've been told many men prefer this over being led to believe another date is going to happen—only to be met with silence when they propose one.

WHEN YOU'RE INTERESTED

Before you go on the date, decide what your physical boundaries are if the date goes well. Some women won't sleep with a man until they've dated him for a number of months, or even kiss him until a certain amount of time has passed. It's good to be clear before passion (or something else) sweeps you away on the date. That way, you can be sure the first date remains a positive experience for you, and you won't have regrets in the morning.

When it's over, tell him you had a nice time and would like to see him again. Don't be coy about this. Be direct. Dr. Papadopoulos says, "Say what you mean. Don't hold back because you're afraid being excited to see him again will put him off. If he likes you, he'll be thrilled and relieved by your honesty. If it scares him off, he wasn't right for you from the start."

The Ups and Downs of Dating

You buy a cute shirt, put on some lipstick (if you remember what that is), and agree to meet a man for coffee. The conversation flows effortlessly and easily, he touches your arm a few times, he makes you laugh, you feel a funny feeling in your stomach that you don't recognize (hint: it's giddiness, not indigestion), and then he walks you to your car. "I had a great time," he says, "Let's do it again."

"Okay," you agree. And you promptly call all your friends to tell them about your new boyfriend. Day one passes without a call. Day two and three reveal no text, no email, nothing from the man. You're sure he's been killed in a terrible accident, but then you see his profile is still online (and active). You hate to admit that you're not entirely relieved to find out he's still alive.

On day four, you give up hope and call your friends crying. "What the hell happened? We had such a good time! I don't understand." Your friends will console and reassure you in all the ways they know how. They'll say he's a jerk and doesn't deserve you. They'll say you'll meet someone else soon. And all of this is true. But what's also true is that dating can unhinge the stabilizing work and growth you've accomplished since your divorce.

When I first started dating, any form of rejection seemed devastating. After going on a date twice with a man only to have him say he couldn't see me anymore, I called Jill, crying. "What's wrong with me? I didn't even know his last name, why am I so upset about this?"

"Because it reminds you of all of the pain and hurt from your marriage. It's rejection all over again. It's not about him, it just opened up your old wounds."

I had very limited dating experience, so I took these "rejections" personally. After a friend kindly explained the principles of dating to me, the first one being that dating often involved seeing several people at the same time, it became less devastating for me when a man didn't call me for a second date. Paul Brunson, author of, *It's Complicated (But It Doesn't Have to Be)*, suggests viewing rejection as an opportunity to seek out someone else. He claims dating is about volume: the more opportunities you expose yourself to, the better your chances are of success.

My confidence grew stronger, and I learned how to shrug off the early dates that didn't work out. But then I stumbled upon another hazard of dating. I'd date a man for a few months and feel close to him. He'd claim the same, and then the following night, he'd say, "I can't do this anymore." Jill, once again my mentor, explained this as the "I didn't plan on caring about you" conundrum. I refuted her theory, saying, "Why would you date someone with the intention of not caring about them?"

"So you don't get hurt," was her reply. And sure enough, several men I dated verified her theory. They explained that yes, they wanted to care about someone, but not so much that they could possibly get hurt. And one really honest man said, "I always make sure the woman likes me more. That way when it ends, I'm not left in a heap."

Yes, this hurt my feelings as well as baffled me. But it also taught me a lot about dating, other people, and most importantly, who I was, what my values were and what I wanted.

Leave Your Kids Out of Your Dating Life

For the first year and a half of dating, I kept all of my partners separate from my kids. If my daughter asked who I was talking to on the phone, I told her, "my friend Greg," but I didn't invite Greg to come to the beach with us or have dinner with us. I knew I was experimenting and that these relationships were short-term. The dates were for me, not my kids. I limited my date nights to the evenings that my kids were at their father's and tried to keep the phone chatting and texting to a minimum when I was with my kids.

Genevieve Clapp, author of *Divorce and New Beginnings*, says, "The key when you have children is to *go slowly*. Give them time to adjust to their family's collapse before you introduce another person into their lives." Clapp reiterates what therapist Tanya Valenti said, which is that children can usually only deal with one big change at a time. Transitioning from your house to your ex's is a large enough change for them to endure. I recommend holding off on introducing them to any man until they've had time to adjust to the divorce and have had a period of stability.

While you are experimenting and getting to know what you want and need, be as present for your kids as possible. They need a stable, available mom more than ever. Try to leave the sexy texting, long phone calls with men, and nights away from your kids to a minimum. And please don't include them in any of your dating drama. If a man dumps you or doesn't return your calls, call a friend. Don't cry about this to your kids or even share it with them. Let them be kids, not your therapist.

At the same time, don't hide your emotions from your kids, because they may think you're upset with them. It's all right to say you're upset about something someone did, or that you're disappointed that your plans didn't work out and you need a few minutes of privacy to call a friend. Make sure your kids know it has absolutely nothing to do with them and that you'll be available as soon as you finish your phone call. This way, you are telling them what they already know—that you're upset—without burdening them with details that they do not need.

By reassuring them that your emotional state has nothing to do with them, they learn that it's all right for Mom to have her varied emotions because she knows how to handle her emotions effectively. Being present with them after you talk to a friend or cry in your room for a few minutes helps ensure they won't feel nervous or responsible for you when you're upset, because you return to them as soon as you're done. As long as you don't make your kids your caretakers; don't let them think your anger or sadness is their fault when it's not; and are emotionally present for them as often as you can be, you are showing them healthy ways to deal with emotions.

CHAPTER 13

RELATIONSHIPS VERSUS RELATIONSHIPS

AFTER A YEAR OF DATING, I found myself back in my therapist's office. "I think I'm ready for something more than casual dates," I confessed.

"Great, so you're ready for a relationship?"

While I sputtered and squirmed in my seat, she explained the difference between a relationship and a Relationship. "Little *r* means maybe you want to talk a few times a week. Maybe he spends the night sometimes. You think about introducing him to your kids..." I gasped at this one.

"Okay, maybe he doesn't meet the kids yet, but maybe someday he will," she said.

"I might be open to that. What's the other kind of relationship?"

"Relationship with a big *R* is one where you start to imagine your future together and..."

"Say no more, I'm not ready for that."

And thus, I embarked on the road to navigating a relationship. With a little *r*.

Be Honest With Yourself and Others

Relationship expert John Gray says being able to think about your ex without pain and in a peaceful way is a signal you are ready to get involved with someone new. This isn't to say you won't ever get triggered again—you will, but it's merely a suggestion that you be as honest as you can about where you are emotionally. Entering new relationships often triggers old hurts, anger, and fears that you think you are healed from. Admit this to yourself—and your partners—when this happens, and try to move through it. If he is scared off by this information, it's better for you to know that early on. You need to be free to heal at your own rate and not be judged or restricted in doing so.

Get Emotionally Divorced First

At the same time, if you are still ruled by anger or grief about your divorce, you probably aren't ready for a significant relationship. Genevieve Clapp claims being emotionally divorced means you have owned your part in the divorce, no longer have guilt or attachment to your former spouse, and feel whole on your own. She says you aren't ready for a serious, committed relationship until you are emotionally divorced. Following the advice and steps in chapters 1–12 will help you with this process. And remember: filing for a divorce is one thing, but becoming emotionally divorced is an even more complicated and lengthy process, so be patient with yourself.

Laura met her boyfriend a year after her divorce. During the first six months of their relationship, Laura's boyfriend was very patient and understanding about her need to process her divorce. But once they were together for almost a year, he grew weary of her rants and rage against her ex-husband. When she complained about this, I sided with the boyfriend. Although Laura had waited a year before dating, she hadn't spent that time becoming emotionally divorced. Therefore, a lot of her processing occurred once she entered the new relationship. Sure, some of this is likely to occur, but Laura's rage still dominated most of her thoughts and conversations. Frankly, I was surprised her boyfriend listened for as long as he did.

Others jump into a new relationship as a way of *avoiding* becoming emotionally divorced. They don't want to be alone, therefore enter relationships quickly. Dawn Bradley Berry, author of *The Divorce*

Recovery Sourcebook, says rebound relationships are based on neediness rather than choice, and are often used to mask painful emotions that need to be faced. "Those who remarry or recommit quickly out of an unbearable need to escape loneliness are cheating themselves, as well as their new partners, out of the grieving and healing that must necessarily precede the healthy entry into a new committed relationship."

Various Kinds of Relationships

Although my therapist explained what a relationship—little r—meant, I was still very confused about the subject. I viewed relationships as being two things: either a casual sexual relationship or a committed relationship that resembled marriage. Many divorce books jumped from dating to remarriage in three pages, which only increased my confusion. I've subsequently learned there are a variety of ways to have a committed relationship that don't involve remarrying. I view remarrying, especially if you have children, as something that takes years to consider. It's a topic worthy of its own book. This book and chapter aren't about remarrying, but rather about considering entering a romantic relationship. If you are considering melding families and step-parenting, please consult many resources before doing so. And equally important, please consider being in several relationships—little *r* ones—before remarrying.

Rather than entering a serious relationship quickly, which Genevieve Clapp says will be built on shaky ground, she encourages developing deeper relationships but not necessarily ones that will lead to marriage. There are many in-between phases of relationships, such as open relationships; monogamous-yet-casual relationships; a relationship where you meet one another's friends but not children, and lots of other options. Similar to when you started dating, it's imperative that you are very clear about what you want in a relationship. If you want to see the man you're dating every weekend, tell him so. If you want to meet his sister, but aren't ready to bring the kids into the picture, tell him that. The relationship can be anything you want it to be, provided it works for him, too. The key is knowing what you want.

Polyamory/Open Relationships

Several women I know shunned traditional, monogamous relationships after their divorce and began experimenting with polyamory or open relationships. Especially if their spouse cheated on them, polyamory allowed the woman to feel reassured that it wouldn't happen again. "Men roam," Amy said. "At least with polyamory, it's out in the open and I get to experiment as well."

For many women, polyamory allowed them to explore their sexuality openly and, as Applewhite said, participate in "transgressive acts." These women weren't ready to remarry, but they were ready to care about someone and open themselves to something more than what dating allowed. Polyamory, or an open relationship, was their in-between relationship. Although many people create polyamorous families and long-term relationships, most of the newly divorced people I knew experimented with the polyamorous lifestyle for only a year or so.

After Joy's divorce, she started dating women. She had several long-term relationships with women and, in general, dated solely women for several years. To her surprise, she was intrigued by a man she met at her son's school. Once they started dating, she explained her past and said she may still be interested in women. He agreed to this, and over the course of their five-year relationship they had an open relationship, were monogamous at times, blended their families at times, and lived apart at times. They continued to reassess their needs as individuals, a couple, and a family, and made adjustments accordingly.

Contrarily, my friend Abigail entered a polyamorous relationship because the man she was interested in was a part of a polyamorous family. Some of the people were married couples where the wife was involved with the same man my friend Abigail was dating. Other members were single women—again in relationships with the man Abigail was with. The single women, wives, and their husbands and children were all considered part of "the family." During the course of Abigail's time with these people, her boyfriend was in a relationship with as many as six other women. To make things even more complicated, every member of the group needed to meet and approve of any new dating or sexual partner. The logistics and drama around this quickly outweighed the benefits, and Abigail moved on to a less complicated, yet still open relationship.

Do all the experimenting you want, but do it for you, not someone else. If you're not ready to commit solely to one person, polyamory or an open relationship could work well for you. But don't agree to be in any type of relationship that makes you uncomfortable. All relationships should be shaped and molded so they work for both partners. If they don't, it's time to find a new partner.

Although I knew several people who experimented with open relationships and experimented myself, Americans don't prove to be very open to this notion statistically. Steve Brody, PhD, a psychologist in Cambria, Calif., estimates that less than 1% of U.S. adults have some sort of open relationship. Franklin Veaux, 41, an Atlanta-based computer programmer and website developer who also runs a polyamory web site, estimates the number to be more around 4% to 9%.[16]

Although I believe open relationships can be a good way to ease yourself into a committed relationship, they can be difficult to manage emotionally. I viewed my open relationship as a way to challenge my insecurities and attempt to feel confident enough in myself not to care if the man I was in a relationship with dated and was intimate with other women. For about four months, I felt righteously liberated from banal emotions such as jealousy. In reality, I think I was in denial. Although the relationship required an incredible amount of energy and it was too soon after my separation to challenge myself in this way, I'm glad I had the experience. My communication skills improved dramatically and it allowed me to realize that I was more ready for a committed, monogamous relationship than I thought I was.

Focus on What You Want, Not What You Don't Want

My open relationship and probably several of my dating partners were chosen out of my need to experiment. I didn't have a huge list of criteria when choosing these partners because I assumed our time together would be short-lived. But that changed when I was done experimenting and ready to commit. Unfortunately, I wasn't very clear on what I was looking for in a partner and committed relationship, I mostly knew what I *didn't* want. A wise woman once told me, "The universe doesn't hear *no*." If all I was doing was focusing on what I *didn't* want, I'd attract exactly *that* to my life. By saying "no more men with Peter Pan complexes," I would be putting a lot of emphasis on "men with Peter Pan complexes." Therefore, I would probably find myself meeting yet another man who didn't want to grow up.

If most of the men you meet are through an online dating site, read their bios carefully. Many sites ask that you choose what you're looking for, such as: "marriage" "long-term relationship," "sex," "casual dating," or "friendship." I often heard women say they didn't want to put "long-term relationship" on their bio because it scared men away. Do it anyway. If you start a relationship based on lies, it will continue to be based on lies, and you won't have your needs met. You're better than that. You can attract the man you want and have what you want. Once you believe it's possible, that is.

The List

Jill's sister Jane scolded me because she thought I wasn't being selective enough when choosing men. "For starters," she said, "the man needs to have everything you have and more."

"Sounds like you're saying I should have a list or something," I laughed.

"Exactly," she said.

I knew a man who had a list containing such high-caliber attributes such as "big boobs," "red hair," and "smart, but not as smart as me." Therefore, I viewed lists as shallow and had never created one. But not having one wasn't working too well for me, so I decided to follow Jane's suggestion. I brainstormed such attributes as a career he was interested in and successful at, physical health, emotional health (or at least a willingness to address his issues), creative pursuits or interests, and close friendships. I didn't care about his salary, but I did want him to be financially responsible. I don't like to drive, so wanted the man to live within five miles of me. I increased the age range to my age and up to twelve years older than I. As for physical descriptions, I'd been attracted to a wide range of men, so I emphasized chemistry over their specific physical attributes. I was ambivalent about whether or not I wanted to date a dad, so I remained open to both dads and men who were childless.

I met a couple of fathers, but those relationships didn't go anywhere. The chemistry wasn't great and I think they were still mourning their divorces. I was very attracted to a contractor with two teen daughters who'd taken a year off to write a book. He was smart, funny, sweet, handsome, and creative. And also moving to Africa. That ended that.

And then online, I came across a childless man with a fuzzy picture but an interesting bio. I emailed him, he emailed back, and we continued this for a couple of weeks. He didn't live five miles from me. He actually lived sixty miles away, but I agreed to meet him for coffee anyway. On our first date I learned he smoked, something akin to being an ax-murderer in Seattle, but I agreed to a second date anyway. "So much for my list," I thought to myself.

In her book, *Marry Him: The Case for Settling for Mr. Good Enough*, Lisa Gottlieb also followed a married friend's advice to create a list of attributes and criteria she desired in a partner. "Off the top of her head," Gottlieb said she listed more than 60 criteria the man must have. Over 60! Although I agreed with many of her criteria, many were trivial—if not outrageous—such as "over five feet ten, but under six feet" and "not into sci-fi." I viewed ruling a man out because he didn't fit her very limited height requirements as absurd. Her list was even more limiting because it was full of "but not…" such as "quirky but not weird." Following all of her desires with a "but not" made her already extremely difficult-to-achieve list all the more difficult. It also was putting a lot of "no" energy into a list that should instead be full of positive attributes.

Gottlieb dismissed many men merely because they didn't have enough criteria on her list, only to later realize they may have satisfied her in more ways than people who *did* have a lot of the criteria she was supposedly looking for. "Lists are also confusing because they're about qualities a man has independently, but fail to take into account qualities he'll have in a relationship," she said.

Focus on the Relationship, Not the List

The clearer Gottlieb became about what she wanted from a relationship, the smaller her list became. By focusing on what was important versus what was superficial, she was open to dating a larger variety of men. She started a relationship with a man who failed miserably according to her list, but excelled in real life. Their relationship met her primary needs by being filled with humor, intellectual stimulation, shared values, and physical chemistry. Her *needs* were met, even without most of her list *criteria* being met. So she changed her advice to "dump the list, not the man."

The clearer I became about what I wanted in a relationship, the smaller my list became. My focus shifted away from the man and more to how *I felt* around the man. Feeling heard, respected, cherished, and interested in the man began to trump where he lived and his hobbies. Movies and romance novels have perpetuated the myth of falling in love with the perfect person. I don't know anyone who is perfect, nor do I think anyone should be perfect, so I tried to remove that fantasy from my brain. Believing that there is a "perfect soul mate" for us can cause us to overlook many potential partners who we could have meaningful relationships with. Maybe he's not perfect, but chances are, we aren't either.

Sheila Ellison, author of *Courage to Love Again*, says our expectations for ourselves and our relationships can either work for or against us. "When we set reasonable expectations that spring from a balanced place, then those expectations can help guide and direct our choices. If the expectations we set cause us to be unhappy, feeling that we aren't good enough or that our life isn't the way we need it to be, then they work against you..." She says after divorce, the key is to try "to be sure that our expectations are built on a foundation of self-love and healthy relationship patterns."

What's Your Love Language?

Understanding your communication style and "love language" can help you communicate your expectations as well as have your needs met in a relationship. According to author Gary Chapman, there are five ways ("love languages") people communicate love: words of affirmation, quality time, gifts, acts of service, and physical touch. Figure out what your love language is and let the man you are in a relationship with—or want to be in a relationship with—know this. Learn about his love language as well and experiment with ways to meet one another's needs. If you aren't speaking the same language, chances are neither of you is feeling heard, validated, or loved.

Holding eye contact when a person is talking, giving undivided attention, and responding to what the person says without negating it all fall under the "quality time" love language. I need that above all else from my relationships. "Good listening skills" became my main list criteria when choosing men and the attribute that often enhanced or ended my relationship.

Avoid Waiting

Knowing when to enter a relationship is tricky, but not nearly as complicated as making a relationship work. Once the honeymoon phase is over, you will most likely experience problems. Problems are not necessarily deal breakers; what matters is how we deal with them—or don't deal with them. Learning how to compromise is necessary, but knowing what to compromise on and what not to can be difficult.

Mira Kirshenbaum in her book, *Too Good to Leave, Too Bad to Stay*, says to avoid the waiting trap of hoping the man will change, and instead try to let go of the perceived problem yourself. Obviously, some problems such as being abusive should not be tolerated. But other problems, like things that merely irritate you or you don't like, can be let go. She says, "If you can really let go of the problem that's most making you feel you want to leave your partner, if you can stop paying attention to it or stop letting it bother you, there's a real chance this relationship is too good to leave."

After her marriage, Mary entered a relationship with a man fifteen years older than she. Although her friends cautioned that she would resent her partner for not being as physically fit and able as she was—or even worse, that she would become his caretaker—the relationship offered her an emotional connection far deeper than any of her previous relationships, so she continued it. When her partner refused to properly address his diabetes and other health concerns, she nagged and scolded him. This caused tension in the relationship, and Mary thought it was going to lead to a break-up. With help from her therapist, she learned to let go of trying to control and change her partner's style of dealing with his health issues and instead trust that he was a grown man who could take care of himself. In doing so, the relationship was deemed "too good to leave" and they continued to live together happily for several more years.

I knew from my marriage that waiting and hoping for someone to change only led to resentment. When I first started dating, I usually let go of the relationship rather than hoping the man and relationship would change. I had a record playing continually in my head and it said, "I'm not married to this man, I don't share kids with this man, so I don't have to deal with any of his bullshit." Not putting up with "bullshit" was my way of reassuring myself that I wouldn't stay in a relationship past the point I should leave.

Over time, I learned to create a "let go" pile, a "don't know how to deal with this yet" pile, and a "non-negotiable" pile. In order to create these piles, I had to be able to decipher what was my business and what wasn't. In my early relationships, I viewed everything as my business, and everything affected me. Over time, I learned how to stop viewing it this way. For instance, with the man who smoked and lived far away, I could have viewed his smoking as something that affected me because secondhand smoke has ill effects. But really, it was none of my business. He smoked outside, never stuck a cigarette in my mouth, and quit when he was ready, probably because I didn't nag him about it.

I was aware that all relationships involved problems and compromise, and that my life and schedule as a forty-year-old mother was complicated and demanding, so I expected the same complications in my partner's life. But how he coped with these complications and stress, how and if he made time to include me emotionally and physically, how he treated and valued his children, and most of all how he communicated were clear indicators to whether the relationship was viable for me. If he didn't communicate well, shut me out, didn't parent responsibly, or coped with everyday problems in unhealthy ways, I viewed this as an excessive amount of "bullshit," and these were areas that I couldn't let go of.

If he was working on the issues himself, I stayed in the relationship. I didn't try to convince him to work on the issues or try to change him, because I knew that would only lead to resentment. I do believe people can change, but only if they want to. They need to be in charge of their change and motivated to change in order for it to work. Trying to change for someone else is more difficult and often leads to resenting the person who made the demand. The key is to understand your own capacity to change and your partner's capacity and willingness early on in the relationship. From there, you can either accept his willingness and limitations, or move on.

Bottom Lines

I don't believe in ultimatums, but I do believe in having bottom lines for myself. Obviously, any physical, sexual, or emotional abuse should be a bottom line for everyone. Destructive behavior towards oneself or others should also be a bottom line. People vary on their acceptance levels, so it's up to you to create your other bottom lines.

Mira Kirshenbaum says these bottom lines are the key to knowing when you should stay in a relationship and when you should leave. She says people who were happy with their relationship knew when and if their partner crossed that line they "were willing to act on that knowledge." She goes on to say, "Not acknowledging your bottom lines and not acting when they're violated has permanently damaging psychological consequences."

Having bottom lines allowed me to stop obsessing about an issue and stop trying to control the other person. It put the responsibility back on me, where it needed to be. If and how the man addressed my bottom line no longer mattered as much, because I was clear on what I would do and when I would do it if my bottom line wasn't adhered to. I didn't try to control him; I merely asked for what I needed.

Bottom Lines are not Ultimatums

Be careful not to confuse ultimatums with bottom lines, because they are two very different creatures. Ultimatums are when you insert your will upon another. When Lily's boyfriend refused to address his anger issues she said, "I'm going to break up with you if you don't see a therapist about your problems." That's an ultimatum, and ultimatums rarely work. Even if her boyfriend agreed to see a therapist, he probably wouldn't have benefitted from the experience because he would have attended the sessions only to appease Lily. Even worse, he didn't see a therapist, but Lily never broke up with him. Instead, she continued to be angry and resentful about his anger problem.

Your bottom lines are about you, not your boyfriend. In Lily's case, a bottom line could have been, "I can't accept you coming home from work yelling at me and then punching the wall." "Don't yell at me and be physically violent" is an acceptable bottom line, but asking someone to never be angry or address their anger issues according to your plan is trying to get *them* to change. Claiming you are going to break up with them if they don't do it is manipulative. Stating an ultimatum, but then not following through with it, is even worse. It could make you lose respect in yourself and your word. Your partner may stop respecting you as well and not believe you mean what you say, because you didn't follow through with your threat.

Your bottom line is a deal you make with *yourself*. An ultimatum is a deal you demand from someone else. Create your bottom lines *for yourself*, not as a way to try to change someone. State them to your partner once or twice, but do not continue to remind him, cajole him, or nag him. If you nag, you're trying to control. He is free and should create his own bottom lines as well. This allows you both to feel heard, respected, and confident that you are having your needs met.

If a bottom line was crossed inadvertently—before it was communicated—then decide if you can accept that and him or if you need to leave. Punishing him or trying to make him earn your trust back or "make it up to you" in other ways is manipulative. If you need to take some time to figure out if you are going to stay or leave, that's fine, but tell him what you're doing. Merely withdrawing from him and shutting down physically or emotionally is punitive and not going to get you what you want, which is a connected, trusting relationship.

"Before we close down we need to ask ourselves what we are hoping to accomplish by shutting down," Melody Beattie says in *The Language of Letting Go*. "Do we need some time to deal? To heal? To grow? To sort things out? Do we need time away from this relationship? Or are we reverting to our old ways—hiding, running, and terminating relationships because we are afraid we cannot take care of ourselves in any other way?"

Put the Trust Where it Needs to Be

I was the poster child for shutting down when I was afraid I wouldn't get my needs met. And guess what? It always resulted in not having my needs met. It was self-sabotage, but I didn't know how to feel safe any other way. Nagging also created distance and tension in my relationships. Having bottom lines allowed me to stop these negative coping mechanisms. It allowed me to put the trust back where it needed to be, with *me*, so I didn't feel the need to control, nag, or manipulate my partner.

Countless women told me they didn't trust men, so they refused to be in a relationship. But in actuality, they didn't trust themselves or feel secure enough to know they would make healthy choices and take action to protect themselves before their relationship became unsafe or detrimental.

Yes, divorce can shatter our confidence in ourselves, as well as our perceptions. We assumed our marriages would last, and many of us were blind to some of the problems that surfaced. So we became terrified of being blind—or blindsided—again. Some of us think the solution to this lies in choosing the "right" partner. But someone who seems right one month can end up incredibly wrong the next month. Instead, we need to put that responsibility on ourselves to be wise enough to learn from our mistakes and grow and change from them. We are the only variable we can control, so we need to focus on ourselves and our ability to change, not on others.

Repeating the Past

It is human nature to repeat patterns because they are what we know. These patterns are familiar, even if they're uncomfortable. This means we often find ourselves in similar relationships with different people. According to Harville Hendrix, Ph.D., founder of Imago Relationship Therapy and author of nine books, including *Getting the Love You Want*, people seek partners who remind them, both positively and negatively, of their primary caretakers. They do not do this consciously, but rather are drawn to people who feel familiar. This is called looking for our "Imago match."

David Richo, author and psychotherapist, claims repetition is not only human nature, it's nature's nature. Seasons repeat themselves, every day has a dawn and a dusk, and yes, women often date the same type of man over and over again. Before you give up on relationships and instead commit yourself to donuts, know that both Hendrix and Richo claim that this repetition does not necessarily have to be a bad thing. Richo says in his book *When the Past is Present*, "Repetition helps us get through things… Repetition helps us resolve the past, but only if we are so conscious of it that we can process it and let it go." And Hendrix claims that our "Imago match" relationships present us with the opportunity to heal past wounds and find deep relational fulfillment.

There were many days when I felt as if I were stuck in the movie *Groundhog Day*, continuing to repeat negative patterns and relationships over and over again. Yes, it was tiring and challenging, but incrementally I saw change and progress in my ability to communicate, to be more rational even when I was emotional, to listen to the other person, and to let go of my need to control. I was as committed to my own growth as I was to the men I was with. As long as I was learning and growing, I usually stayed in the relationship. I was willing to endure the long, difficult discussions that arose when someone felt hurt or we couldn't reach an easy compromise, digging deep into my own negative characteristics. I knew if I didn't, I wouldn't ever be able to have the mature Relationship (with a big R) that I yearned for.

Your threshold for owning your part in an argument, willingness to examine yourself and your actions, ability to be vulnerable, and the amount of work you are willing to put into a relationship is up to you to decide. But if you feel as if you're doing the same thing over and over again and not making even incremental improvements, you may want to scrutinize your actions and yourself a little more thoroughly.

When and How to Introduce Your Kids

Before you introduce your kids to a man you're seeing, refer to the person around your kids for some time before the actual introductions. Dawn Bradley Berry suggests in *The Divorce Recovery Sourcebook*, that "a casual, natural approach in which the fact that the parent is seeing new people is not kept secret, but is a separate part of the parent's life."

Over time, when you start to feel as if everyone is ready for the introduction, have a frank conversation with your partner in which you ask him his intentions and hopes for the relationship. Ask him what he thinks the purpose of the introduction is and what role he wants to play in your children's lives. Ask him how active he wants to be in your kids' lives, what he feels comfortable with and what he doesn't. Does he want to parent your kids? Be their friend? None of the above? And what do you want from him? What do you feel comfortable with and what do your kids need? Be certain of your needs and hopes and state them to him so you don't set him up for failure. Check in with your kids as well to see how they feel about a new man entering your life. No, your kids' needs shouldn't dictate your life, but they should be considered when making large decisions, such as introducing them to a new partner.

My kids both claimed, shortly after our separation, that they didn't want a stepmother (thank you, fairy tales, for never having evil stepfathers!). Eventually, my son said he didn't want me to ever remarry. Although at the time remarrying sounded as appealing as sticking pins in my eyes, I knew that may change, so I told him, "I can't say that I'll never marry again, but I can promise you that if and when that ever happens you will have had a long time to get to know the man first. I can also say he would have to fit in with us as a family and understand and accept the way we do things in order for me to even consider being in a relationship with him."

My kids were only three and six when I separated, so they did not have any knowledge of dating or boyfriends. I took their "no remarrying" comment to mean, "We don't want to deal with another man in your life." So when I first started dating, I kept my two worlds separate. Eventually, my kids became more interested in my social life and I became more open to combining my two worlds. My willingness to work on the relationship rather than flee was one of the benchmarks I used when deciding whether or not to introduce the man to my kids. But ultimately, I waited until I felt all of us were ready to meet one another rather than gauging the "first meet" solely on my feelings about the man.

The first man I introduced was someone I loved, but I wasn't sure our relationship would last for very long. Even if the relationship ended in six months, I felt confident that I had protected my kids from seeing men come and go from my life and that the kids and the man were ready to meet. And they were. I, on the other hand, was a nervous wreck. While he played Connect Four in the living room with the kids, I floundered around the house in attempt to calm myself down.

The first time you introduce your kids to a man may be terrifying, but trust me, it gets easier. I learned that it was easier if we all had an activity to focus on (or other people around) so the attention wasn't primarily on meeting my boyfriend. If I wanted the event to be casual, I needed to act casual. I usually invited other kids over to play with my kids during the first introduction so the new boyfriend could see us in as natural an element as possible, rather than all of us staring at him at the dinner table. Dawn Bradley Berry recommends creating a low-pressure atmosphere where little interaction is required. She suggests going to a sporting event, the beach, or somewhere where the spotlight and topic of conversation doesn't need to be solely on the new man.

Once my kids had been introduced to and gotten to know two of my boyfriends, introductions to men were far easier and more casual. I stopped keeping my dating life separate from them and instead had dates pick me up at the house. I told the kids when I was going on a date and described the man if they asked. By then, my kids knew what dating meant and what a boyfriend was. They knew dates were casual, so they rarely asked about the men I dated. They also felt secure that no one would be considered to become a boyfriend if he didn't meld with our family. My kids also knew that no matter if I was dating, in a relationship, or single, they were my priority and I was available to them. They were secure in who their father was and who their mother was, and they knew no one was trying to replace that or take a parent away from them. My boyfriends were always referred to as "my mom's boyfriend," and not thought of as another parent. They liked the men, but they weren't particularly attached to them.

Introducing Teenagers to Your Partner

If you have teenagers, when and how you introduce a new partner will be more complex. Allowing them to have a say—but not the ultimate say—in when and how they meet your partner can be the first step in reassuring them and creating a positive atmosphere. Be careful to not give them too much say, because teens can be surly and wield that power to try to prohibit you from moving on with your romantic life. Your teens are probably still hoping you will get back with your ex. So understand that hope, not spite, may be what fuels their dislike of your new partner. Dawn Bradley Brown says if your kids seem cold to your new partner, "don't push them and, above all, don't worry—confusion and reluctance is quite natural." She claims that most kids end up accepting the new partner, but sometimes that takes as long as a year. In the meanwhile, rude or manipulative behavior should not be accepted, so if this occurs, set guidelines and boundaries. And most importantly, remind your kids continuously that they are loved and will never be replaced by the new partner.

Modeling Healthy Adult Relationships for Your Kids

Part of the reason I wanted to introduce my kids to men, even when I knew I wasn't going to marry them, was because I felt it was my responsibility to show my kids what adult relationships looked like. Jeremy and I had led parallel lives and then divorced when they were young, so we had not shown them this. They didn't learn it at their friends' houses either, because play dates usually ended before the other spouse came home from work. I showed them the affectionate side of relationships by greeting boyfriends with a hug and a kiss, holding hands when we walked, and telling them I loved them in front of the kids. By not shielding all of our disagreements from them, I also showed them how adults worked out their differences. Obviously, anything long or heated took place when the kids weren't there, but some disagreements I chose to work out when they were home to show them how compromises can be made and how to get to the other side of an argument in a healthy manner. And once I was absolutely sure they didn't feel threatened by a boyfriend, I also asked for time and space to talk only to him. This was something Jeremy and I failed at, so my kids sometimes thought the world revolved around them and their own stories. I started off asking for ten minutes for "adult conversation," and then I'd return to them afterward. Soon enough, I didn't have to put a time limit on it, and adult, uninterrupted conversation occurred more naturally.

You may not feel the need to show this to your kids. You may want to introduce your kids only to a man you are going to live with or marry. That's fine, as long as you aren't using your kids as an excuse to not get involved in a relationship or as a way to block a relationship's progress. Sure, if you're newly separated, experiencing another large transition, or your kids are emotionally vulnerable, I recommend waiting before introducing the kids to the man. I recommend waiting as well if your ex is not in your children's lives, and you're worried your kids will become immediately attached to your new boyfriend. But otherwise, know that your kids are probably more resilient than you think. They might not agree at first, but you must trust that your happiness and growth is ultimately what is best for the entire family. Denying your needs is not good for anyone. And the longer your kids become accustomed to you being single, the harder it will be for them to accept you as part of a couple.

If the Relationship Ends

Many women told me they were reluctant to introduce a partner to their children because they were concerned that their children would feel abandoned again if the relationship ended. This is a valid fear. But you can't enter a relationship worrying about the end. If your partner ends up being a significant person in your children's lives, you could consider allowing them to still visit him and spend time with him if the two of you break up. If that feels too difficult and like it will only delay the grieving that needs to take place, you can make a clean break. You'll know what to do when the time comes, so try not to let fear of a potential end derail you from moving forward in your relationship.

I was clear and concise when telling my kids about my break-ups, and I made sure they knew they had absolutely nothing to do with them, because they didn't. As I said, my kids were not very attached to my boyfriends, so they were not very affected by my break-ups either. Their foundation was based on me, each other, and their father, and that didn't change just because my romantic relationships ended. If I missed the person and felt sad and my kids noticed, I told them why I was sad. I didn't process the relationship or its end with my children. I merely explained the reason around my sadness. I called a friend if I needed to process.

Go to Your Cave, but Don't Hide There

Just like you don't want to rush into a relationship right after your divorce, you don't want to rush into someone else's arms right after a break-up. Take some time to heal, reflect, and regain your relationship with yourself. If we try to fill the hole that someone left behind with another person, we only end up with two holes. First, you need to make yourself whole—without a relationship.

I called my alone time between relationships "going into the cave." I loved the cave. It was full of books, lavender bath gel, and pound cake. I also processed a lot there, which was mandatory for my healing. I'd think about patterns I repeated in the relationship, my part in the break-up, and what I hoped to do differently next time. Eventually, the processing minimized and serenity set in. I enjoyed spending more time with my friends, having time for myself, and usually started on a project I had been neglecting. Life was often calm and serene in the cave. Being outside of the cave required a lot of work, and trust me, I considered staying inside forever. I romanticized the life of monks and nuns, and thought a life with donuts and solo naps could suit me just fine. I would start to feel smug while hearing and observing others' relationship problems, and I'd think I was above and beyond such troubles. That was my cue to get out of the cave. It was easy for me to be serene and smug while alone in the cave. The key was for me to learn how to be serene and secure in myself *all of the time.*

When I asked my friend Diane why she had been single for five years, she said, "Fear, obviously!"

Yes, we've been hurt. Yes, we may even get hurt again, but we should not take up permanent residence in the cave due to fear. If you are not willing to take risks, you aren't moving on. That's why I suggest taking time to heal and process your past relationships and your part in the break-up, but once you've done so, it's time to get out there again. Daring to be in a relationship again can help you heal in ways that are difficult to do while alone.

A woman interviewed in *The Courage to Love* described it this way: "It is sad when love dies, but it is so glorious when it is alive. I learn so much about myself when I'm in a relationship. I grow, I am challenged to work on some of my bad habits, and I learn about the other person's life, problems, and bad habits." Try to adopt this woman's outlook by remembering yes, daring to love again can hurt, but it can also lead to joy and growth.

After her divorce, Hope took a couple of years to focus on her kids and career. While in her cave, she also discovered hobbies such as knitting and photography. Life was good in the cave for the most part, but every once in a while she yearned for more. Whether it was sex or mere male companionship, something would lure her out of the cave. She'd accept a date from a colleague or put her profile on a dating site. Some of the dates were duds, but a few of them turned into second, third, and twelfth dates. When the dates turned to a committed relationship, Hope would end it. "I always ended it before he did so I wouldn't get hurt." And back to her cave she would go.

By supposedly protecting herself, Hope was actually harming herself. By ending the relationship before it had a chance, she was sealing her fate of being alone rather than being willing to risk that a relationship might work out. For years, she told herself she was happy, but one day she opened her closet and over a hundred scarves and hats that she'd knitted fell out. "No one needs that many hats," she said, laughing. Two of her children had moved out and one was about to graduate from high school. "Did I really want to be left alone with my hats?" she questioned. "No," was the answer, but how to change that destiny was complicated. She had relied on her coping mechanism of ending relationships quickly for so many years that changing would not come easily or instantly. But recognizing the issue and knowing it was no longer serving her were the first steps she needed to make a change.

While in your cave, ask yourself what you're doing there. Are you healing and taking time to sort out your wants, thoughts, and desires? Great! Stay there for as long as you need. Are you merely enjoying being single after so many years of being in a relationship? Great again! Focus on yourself rather than others for a while. Or are you hiding and avoiding intimacy? If so, get out of the cave. You don't need to go on a date, but you should at least call a girlfriend and meet her for dinner or a walk. The reruns of *Law and Order* and your yarn will always be there next weekend. Socializing with real people may benefit you more this weekend. Even if it is scary.

Chapter 14

Remember the Big Picture

YES, I ENCOURAGE YOU TO DATE and risk love again, but I don't want to suggest it should become your sole focus. Many of us lost more than our husbands in the years leading to the divorce, so I encourage you to remember and celebrate everything you've *gained* since the divorce. Perhaps you have strengthened your friendships or made new friends. Or you've changed jobs and are now challenged and fulfilled in a way you weren't before. Maybe you've increased your confidence by learning how to ask for what you need. Or you've taken up sewing, kickboxing, belly dancing, or skydiving. Or you've remodeled your house, or merely bought some beautiful pillows for your bed. Maybe you have time to read now, and garden, and really listen to your children. Bask in these accomplishments and celebrate them. No matter how trivial they seem, they are worth celebrating because you made them happen for yourself. Even if you are in a new loving, healthy relationship, please remember to appreciate all of the other things you have changed or gained since your divorce, along with your new love.

Focus On What You Have

It's very easy for us to focus on what we don't have. But I hope you can focus on what you *do* have. Whenever I called my friend Cedar with a problem, she listened, and then suggested I make a gratitude list. I used to resist this notion. I didn't want to be grateful,

I wanted to complain! But I learned how effective it was at shifting my scarcity mentality into abundance. No matter how terrible my day or situation was, my gratitude list was always far more extensive than my complaint list. My friends, kids, health, and career were always on my gratitude list, but I also added small things such as "the crocus blooming in my yard" or "the joke my son told at dinner." After a round of insomnia, Ambien was put on my gratitude list. The list doesn't need to be noble or deep. Anything and everything is acceptable.

The gratitude lists helped shift my tendency to focus on what was next, or the thing I didn't have, rather than take time to appreciate what I did have and where I currently was. As my friend Cindy explained, "You and I view all of our accomplishments as little hills we've walked over rather than mountains we've climbed. Even worse, we're constantly focused on the next, bigger mountain. But once we climb that mountain, it's merely deemed a hill as well."

I knew Cindy was right, so I tried to manage the impact my restlessness and drive had on my life. If my drive was helping my career or my restlessness caused me to learn a new skill, those instincts served me. But if I was feeling discontent and obsessed with what I didn't have, I learned to say "yet." Saying "yet" reminded me that whatever my lack or emptiness was at that moment, it wasn't permanent. Even more important was remembering that I wasn't the almighty person in charge of every aspect of my life and destiny. Sure I wanted this thing now! I always wanted things now, and I falsely assumed the harder I tried, the sooner I could have that thing NOW. But great strides in my career and fabulous romantic relationships didn't happen merely because I wanted them (now!) Often, good things happened when I stopped fixating on them.

This isn't to say I sat back eating bonbons while waiting for the perfect book deal or man to knock on my door. I simply learned when to stop forcing the issue. I didn't pretend I didn't want these things, but they weren't the main things I focused on. I stopped measuring the quality of my life on whether or not I had these things and instead saw my life for all that it had: many good things, a few things I was changing, and even fewer things I didn't have (yet). It also allowed me to accept the things I couldn't change as being just that: things I couldn't change.

Focusing on what I didn't have also caused a lot of unnecessary worry. While at my son's counselor's office one day (a great place to worry), I saw the words "Worrying is like praying, only for bad things" written on the bathroom wall. After laughing out loud, I committed this profound graffiti to memory. The graffiti helped me learn how to feel my feelings, but then move on. "Okay," I'd say to myself, "go ahead and worry for ten minutes." Once I fully expressed my concerns in my journal or otherwise, it was easier to then say, "And now, think about all of the things you worried about before that either never happened, or did happen and it was for the best." Almost all of my past worries fell into one of these categories.

Honor Your Path

My path towards divorce and afterward didn't always make sense, and it wasn't easy or even successful all the time. But it's the path that got me where I am today, so I wouldn't change it. I could (and still can) honestly answer the question, "Do you have any regrets about your divorce?" with a vehement, "No!"

I spent two years after my divorce writing another memoir, only to never submit it. I made and lost some friends, I failed and succeeded in many work attempts, and I spent a lot of weekends feeling joyful and grateful while other weekends I felt sad or scared. My efforts sometimes seemed frivolous or futile at the time, but they all furthered larger goals of learning to forgive, respect, and trust myself. This work helped me get where I am now, which is a very good place emotionally, spiritually, and financially. Healing isn't easy, but I hope you can look back at the difficult times and see the purpose and benefits of them. They helped you get where you are right now.

Even if where you are now doesn't feel like a beautiful place, it will be. And it will feel so sooner if you can focus your energy on being healthy rather than being happy. Our generation puts an extreme amount of pressure on being happy, but as my friend Dusty recently said, "I think happy is nebulous bullshit that can't really be obtained."

"Happy" can be elusive, and often people's expectation of it isn't realistic. It's impossible to be happy all the time, and that shouldn't be our goal. A more realistic goal might be acquiring or honing the ability to feel all our feelings and knowing how to manage the uncomfortable ones. Or perhaps a better goal is striving for being content and healthy rather than eternal happiness. Follow Sheila Ellison's advice about managing our expectations (chapter 13). Our expectations can either work for us or against us, and the goal is to have them work for us so we can feel good about ourselves and our lives.

You Have Options

Ideally, we learn how to be content in and out of relationships. I'm not suggesting you resign yourself to being alone forever. I'm merely saying it's all right not to be in a relationship for a while. If you're lonely, perhaps you could call a friend, take the kids on a fun outing or snuggle with them while reading to them, schedule a massage, treat yourself to a spa, or even call a male friend "with benefits" if it comes to that. You have options, and it's very important to remember that.

Becoming divorced gave me options after years of feeling as if I didn't have many and the ones I did have were bad. I tried to remember my newfound choices whenever I felt stuck or deprived. I also learned to view my breaks between relationships as gifts, because they were. They were a time for me to concentrate on myself, work, my kids, friends, and hobbies. Often, breaks were an opportunity to rest and stop climbing hills. My best and most dedicated writing occurred when I wasn't in a relationship. I also took the best vacations of my life while alone. It was so decadent to do what I wanted, whenever I wanted while in a warm, tropical environment. Jill's sister Jane, who had been married for over twenty years, told me very early in my divorce to cherish my "me" time because I had the rest of my life to be an "us" again. I dismissed her and thought, "Easy for you to say," but years later, I offered the same advice to friends.

Are You In Love With Being In Love?

If you really want to be in a relationship, be in one, but please take time to notice if you're more enthralled with the idea of a relationship than with the actual man. After being with a man for over a year, I confessed to my therapist, "I think I love the idea of being in love more than I love him." She nodded sagely, telling me she had sensed that a while ago.

It was harder to let go of the partnership than it was the actual man because I didn't want to go back to being "alone." Over time, I realized I was more alone in that relationship than I would be on my own. I was pretending I was fulfilled when I really wasn't. And the sooner I let him and our relationship go, the better chance I had of being in love with an actual man, not with the idea of love. My ultimate goal of being in a healthy, fulfilling relationship was actually plausible, but not while I was in love with an idea, not a person. Being alone paradoxically helped me *not* be alone more than being in my current relationship did.

When friends asked me how I was able to end my relationships cleanly and not get back together with the man over and over again, I said, "I don't give up on hope, I just put it where it needs to be. I stop hoping the partner or relationship will change and instead start hoping I can heal enough in order to attract the relationship and partner I'm yearning for."

Hope, like restlessness, can motivate you as well as debilitate you. As long as the hope is directed towards yourself and your ability to change, it will probably benefit your life. When you change, the people you are attracted to and who are drawn to you also change. The healthier and clearer you become, the healthier and clearer your future partners will be. Like attracts like. Remain hopeful about yourself, but give yourself breaks to just be you as you currently are as well.

Divorce Can Lead to Opportunities

My goal was to enjoy all of my phases: being single, dating, relationships, and Relationships. I tried not to have one of these trump or negate the others. I didn't get divorced because I wanted to be in a different relationship. I became divorced because I needed to make a change in my life. That change spurred many other positive changes. I shed my inhibitions about writing and published two books.

I became an established editor and writing coach. I gained confidence in myself as a writer and woman. I became a more present mother. I took risks. I learned to trust myself and love myself. Equally important, I learned to let others help me.

I assumed my divorce would be an end, which it was, but I had no idea that it would also lead to so many beginnings and opportunities as well. My new circle of support, achievements, and emotional health surpass the losses I suffered from divorce. You may not see that in your own life right now, and that's fine. The loss of your marriage needs to be mourned. But believe me when I say one day some good will start to balance out that loss. And when you're ready, opportunities will be available to you. Take advantage of them, and remember to congratulate yourself every step of the way.

FOOTNOTES

1   Brinig, Margaret and Douglas Allen (2000). "These Boots Are Made for Walking: Why Most Divorce Filers Are Women." American Journal of Law and Economics Vol. 2: 126–169.

2   Anato, Paul R., Laura S. Loomis and Alan Booth. "Parental divorce, marital conflict, and offspring well-being during early childhood," *Social Forces* 73 (3) (1995): 895–916.

3   Bauserman, Robert. "Child Adjustment in Joint-Custody Versus Sole Custody Arrangements: A Meta-analytic Review," *Journal of Family Psychology*, 16 (2002): 91–102.

4   del Rosso, Lisa. "Saying I Don't to Release the Anger." *The New York Times*. January 23, 2011.

5   Kübler-Ross, Elisabeth. *On Grief and Grieving: Finding the Meaning of Grief through the Five Stages of Loss*. New York: Simon & Schuster Ltd, 2005.

6   Fisher, Helen. *Why We Love: The Nature and Chemistry of Romantic Love*. New York: Holt. 2004.

7   Carstensen, Laura, L. "Social and emotional patterns in adulthood: Support for socio- emotional selectivity theory." *Psychology and Aging*, 7 (1992): 331–338.

8   Hendrix, Harville Ph.D. *Getting the Love You Want: A Guide for Couples.* New York: Henry, Holt & Co., 2007.

9   U.S. Census Bureau. "Remarriage in the United States," Rose M. Kreider. Poster presented at the annual meeting of the American Sociological Association, Montreal, August10–14, 2006.
http://www.census.gov/hhes/socdemo/marriage/data/sipp/us-remarriage-poster.pdf

10   Wilcox, Christie. "Understanding Our Bodies: Serotonin, The Connection Between Food and Mood." *Nutrition Wonderland,* June 24, 2009. Accessed 1/23/13.
http://nutritionwonderland.com/2009/06/understanding-bodies-serotonin-connection-between-food-and-mood/

11   Luscombe, Belinda. "Who Needs Marriage? A Changing Institution." *Time Magazine,* November 18, 2010. Accessed 5/13/12.
http://www.time.com/time/magazine/article/0,9171,2032116,00.html#ixzz1mILSG8xH

12   CBS News. "Study: Women new financial winners after divorce." Last modified January 18, 2012.
http://www.cbsnews.com/8301-505268_162-57360957/study-women-new-financial-winners-after-divorce/

13   Huffpost Divorce: Marriages Come and Go But Divorce is Forever. "Second, Third Marriages: Divorce Rates Explained." Last modified June 9, 2013.
http://www.huffingtonpost.com/2012/03/06/second-third-marriages-divorce-rate_n_1324496.html

14   Rosenbloom, Stephanie. "Love, Lies and What They Learned," *The New York Times,* November 12, 2011. Accessed June, 11, 2013.
http://www.nytimes.com/2011/11/13/fashion/online-dating-as-scientific-research.html?pagewanted=all&_r=0

15   Orat, James. "Online Dating Statistics," *webcontent.com*. Last
      modified June 22, 2006.
      http://www.webcontent.com/articles/153/1/Online-Dating-
      Statistics/Page1.html

16   Doheny, Kathleen. "The Truth About Open Marriage." Accessed
      May 30, 2012.
      http://www.webmd.com/sex-relationships/features/the-
      truth-about-open-marriage

References

Applewhite, Ashton. *Cutting Loose: Why Women Who End Their Marriages Do So Well*. New York: HarperPerennial, 1998.

Beattie, Melody. *The Language of Letting Go*. Minnesota: Hazeldon, 1990.

Birnbach, Lawrence, Dr. and Hyman, Beverly, Dr. *How to Know if It's Time to Go*. New York: Sterling, 2010.

Botwinick, Amy. *Congratulations on Your Divorce*. Florida: Heath Communications Inc., 2005.

Bradley Berry, Dawn. *The Divorce Recovery Sourcebook*. New York: McGraw Hill, 1999.

Bram, Jessica. *Happily Ever After Divorce: Notes of a Joyful Journey*. Florida: Heath Communications Inc., 2009.

Browning, Dominique. "Alone Again, Naturally." *New York Times*, January 8, 2012.

Buchbinder, Amnon. "Out of Our Heads: Phillip Shepherd On The Brain In Our Belly." *The Sun*, 448 (April, 2013): 7-14.

Brunson, Paul Carrick. *It's Complicated (But It Doesn't Have to Be)*. New York: Penguin Group, 2012.

Chapman, Gary. *5 Love Languages: The Secret to Love that Lasts.* Illinois: Northfield Publishing, 2010.

Clapp, Genevieve, Ph.D. *Divorce and New Beginnings.* New York: John Wiley & Sons, Inc., 2000.

Ellison, Shela. *The Courage to Love Again: Creating Happy, Healthy Relationships after Divorce.* New York: HarperCollins, 2002.

Emory, Robert, Ph.D. *The Truth about Children and Divorce.* New York: Plume, 2006.

Falk, Florence. *On My Own: The Art of Being a Woman Alone.* New York: Three Rivers Press, 2008.

Fisher, Bruce and Alberti, Robert. *Rebuilding: When Your Relationship Ends.* California: Impact Publishers, 2006.

Gadaua, Susan, LCSW. *Contemplating Divorce.* California: New Harbinger Publications, 2008.

Gottlieb, Lori. *Marry Him: The Case for Settling for Mr. Good Enough.* New York: Dutton, 2010.

Gray, John, Ph.D. *Mars and Venus Starting Over.* New York: HarperPerennial, 2002.

Gregory-Thomas, Susan. *In Spite of Everything: A Memoir.* New York: Random House, 2011.

Hayes, Christopher, Ph.D., Anderson, Deborah, and Blau, Melinda. *Our Turn: Women Who Triumph in the Face of Divorce.* New York: Pocket Books, 1994.

Hendrix, Harville Ph.D. *Getting the Love You Want: A Guide for Couples.* New York: Henry, Holt & Co., 2007.

Klinenberg, Eric. *Going Solo: The Extraordinary Rise and Surprising Appeal of Living Alone.* New York: The Penguin Press, 2012.

Kübler -Ross, Elizabeth and Kessler, David. *On Grief and Grieving: Finding the Meaning of Grief through the Five Stages of Loss.* New York: Scribner, 2005.

James, John W. and Friedman, Russell. *The Grief Recovery Handbook.* New York: HarperCollins, 2009.

Lowrance, Michele. *The Good Karma Divorce: Avoid Litigation, Turn Negative Emotions into Positive Actions, and Get On with the Rest of Your Life.* New York: HarperOne, 2011.

MacGregor, Cynthia and Albert, Robert E, Ph.D. *After Your Divorce: Creating the Good Life on Your Own.* California: Impact Publishers, 2006.

Mendelsohn, Daniel. "But Enough about Me." *The New Yorker,* January 25, 2010.

Morrison, Stacy. *Falling Apart in One Piece: An Optimist's Journey through the Hell of Divorce.* New York: Simon and Schuster, 2010.

Papadopoulus, Linda Dr. *What Men Say, What Women Hear: Bridging the Conversation Gap One Conversation At a Time.* New York: Simon Spotlight Entertainment, 2009.

Paul, Pamela. "How Divorce Lost Its Groove." *New York Times,* June, 19, 2011.

Pedro-Carroll, JoAnne. *Putting Children First: Proven Parenting Strategies for Helping Children Thrive Through Divorce.* New York: Penguin, 2010.

Ricci, Isolina. *Mom's House, Dad's House: A Complete Guide for Parents Who Are Separated, Divorced, or Remarried.* New York: Simon and Schuster, 1997.

Richo, David. *When the Past is Present: Healing the Emotional Wounds that Sabotage our Relationship.* Massachusetts: Shambhala Publications, 2008.

Shepherd, Phillip. *New Self, New World: Recovering Our Senses in the Twenty-First Century.* California: North Atlantic Books, 2010.

Strayed, Cheryl. *Wild: From Lost to Found on the Pacific Crest Trail.* New York: Knopf, 2012.

Williams, Alex. "It's Not Me, It's You." *The New York Times*, January, 29, 2012.

Discover more books
and learn about our
new approach to publishing
at **booktrope.com**.

CPSIA information can be obtained
at www.ICGtesting.com
Printed in the USA
FFOW03n1638200814
6960FF

9 781620 153444